WHAT IF I'M WRONG?

AND OTHER KEY QUESTIONS FOR DECISIVE SCHOOL LEADERSHIP

WHAT IF I'M WRONG?

AND OTHER KEY QUESTIONS FOR DECISIVE SCHOOL LEADERSHIP

SIMON RODBERG

ASCD

Alexandria, Virginia USA

1703 N. Beauregard St. • Alexandria, VA 22311-1714 USA
Phone: 800-933-2723 or 703-578-9600 • Fax: 703-575-5400
Website: www.ascd.org • E-mail: member@ascd.org
Author guidelines: www.ascd.org/write

Ranjit Sidhu, *CEO & Executive Director*; Stefani Roth, *Publisher*; Genny Ostertag, *Director, Content Acquisitions*; Susan Hills, *Senior Acquisitions Editor*; Julie Houtz, *Director, Book Editing & Production*; Megan Doyle, *Editor*; Judi Connelly, *Senior Art Director*; Donald Ely, *Associate Art Director*; Cynthia Stock, *Typesetter*; Kelly Marshall, *Manager, Production Services*; Shajuan Martin, *E-Publishing Specialist*

All web links in this book are correct as of the publication date below but may have become inactive or otherwise modified since that time. If you notice a deactivated or changed link, please e-mail books@ascd.org with the words "Link Update" in the subject line. In your message, please specify the web link, the book title, and the page number on which the link appears.

PAPERBACK ISBN: 978-1-4166-2958-0   ASCD product #121009   n8/20
PDF E-BOOK ISBN: 978-1-4166-2960-3; see Books in Print for other formats.
Quantity discounts are available: e-mail programteam@ascd.org or call 800-933-2723, ext. 5773, or 703-575-5773. For desk copies, go to www.ascd.org/deskcopy.

Library of Congress Cataloging-in-Publication Data

Names: Rodberg, Simon, author.
Title: What if I'm wrong? : and other key questions for decisive school
    leadership / Simon Rodberg.
Description: Alexandria, Virginia : ASCD, 2020. | Includes bibliographical
    references and index.
Identifiers: LCCN 2020023544 (print) | LCCN 2020023545 (ebook) | ISBN
    9781416629580 (paperback) | ISBN 9781416629603 (pdf)
Subjects: LCSH: School principals—United States. | Educational
    leadership—United States. | School management and organization—United
    States.
Classification: LCC LB2831.92 .R64 2020 (print) | LCC LB2831.92 (ebook) |
    DDC 371.2/0120973—dc23
LC record available at https://lccn.loc.gov/2020023544
LC ebook record available at https://lccn.loc.gov/2020023545

29 28 27 26 25 24 23 22 21 20   1 2 3 4 5 6 7 8 9 10 11 12

What If I'm Wrong?

And Other Key Questions for Decisive School Leadership

Introduction

It's Hard to Decide

When I was principal, we had a crossing guard—arranged and nominally supervised by the city's transportation department, not by the school—who regularly didn't show up for work. I started to wear an old fluorescent-orange winter jacket in the mornings, just to be prepared. I stood in the middle of an intersection with no traffic lights, with kids and bikes and cars flowing around me, with my cell phone buzzing about which teachers were sick and which classes weren't covered, and tried, in my fluorescent-orange jacket, to make sure neither the children nor I died. I did this on a bunch of mornings. Some days it rained. A couple of times it snowed. I stood waving and pointing and shouting at the kids, at the bikes, at the cars, while doing my best to grin and say hi to everyone who passed.

The 20 minutes of traffic control meant pausing the other things that stuffed up my mornings. The special education coordinator called upset about a suspension; she wanted to talk through the system failures and legal danger and how to use a discipline checklist to do better in the future. A new educational aide, at his first professional employment, requested the day off because his nephew was in mortal danger from gangs in El Salvador; he hadn't yet earned any sick days; how should I treat the request? The school's academic oversight committee was meeting with me at 8:30 to review academic progress, and they wanted to hear about my priorities for the rest of the school year. (I hadn't yet decided on priorities. I was busy directing traffic.) When I headed inside from the intersection after the school day started, at least I could count those 20 minutes as successful principaling: nobody died. Some days I would have rather just been the crossing guard.

How to Think About Decisions

Thinking is not the point of school leadership. The point of school leadership is to make things happen. To make a great school; to graduate happy, intelligent, productive lifelong learners; to retain satisfied, engaged, highly effective teachers; to organize a supportive, active parent community; to produce high test scores, great sports teams, a school play that's both Broadway-quality and has a part for every kid who wants one ...

People who become principals want to make things happen. The problem, as every principal knows—as I found out, over and over again, during my own time as principal—is what things?

That's where thought comes in. Thinking is crucial for *good* school leadership, because figuring out a path through the relentless complexity of our roles is a huge part of school leadership. Thinking is crucial for principals who need to decide—or need to lead their community to decide—what a great school is, how to balance happiness and productivity in their students, who their highly effective teachers are, and when to give in or hold firm with parents. Thinking is crucial to get those high test scores and understand how much to care about them, and to decide whether to attend the school play or the sports championship, to go home to your own children, or just to take a nap!

In the following pages, I'll explore what leads us astray in our decision making and uncover a path toward more thoughtful decisions. The truth is, schools are less intellectual than we'd like to think. They often operate by habit and precedent rather than by careful consideration. They are, despite being nominal centers of learning, prone to every error of the human species: prejudice, groupthink, bad instinct, rush to judgment, and more. Principals are people too, and our shortcomings are exacerbated by work conditions that leave us stressed, overwhelmed, pulled in too many directions to count, and often in need of a full night's sleep.

I want to help you develop a clearer, deeper process that gets you past those moments when you feel most stuck. We don't want just to make things happen; we want specifically those things that align with our vision and values to happen. Being a good crossing guard takes a lot of quick, accurate decisions—so you don't wave cars forward with one hand and wave kids in the same direction with the other—but it's a different kind of thought than a principal's real job requires. Like slow deep breathing, clear deep thinking is harder than it seems, especially for principals barraged with information, questions, and demands on their time.

What Makes Decisions Hard

The intellectual challenge of school-level decision making has many facets. Throughout this book, I'll address specific decision-making errors, how those errors play out in schools, and how to do better. At the start, though, I want only to highlight how big a challenge we confront. Principals want what's best for kids, and of course we err; if people knew what to do better in education, on any consistent basis, they would have done it already! But nobody knows, *really* knows, what to do. School leaders struggle because schools are hard. There is no guidebook containing all the right answers.

School leaders also struggle because schools are important. They are full of vulnerable, yearning, learning human beings. And those are just the teachers! And the teachers are, of course, responsible for young lives, for those young people's futures, and for the future of our country and world as a whole. No wonder decisions are hard; they matter so, so much. The emotional weight of this responsibility can be suffocating. Decisions are hard because, if you are going to do this work right, you care about them so much. I want to help you gain a confidence and clarity in your decision making to match your care.

The truth is, you have to decide. Empathy and an unwillingness to make tough decisions often go together. The caring can get in the way: those who love easily don't want to hurt others because they feel the pain themselves so much. But you can fire somebody with empathy for them, and you can make the decision to fire somebody due to empathy for those affected by the person's poor performance! The right decision should be separated from the impact that is most in front of you. Leadership decisions can't be based on what creates the most interpersonal comfort for the leader. Decision making is hard because it's uncomfortable. If you can't deal with people being mad at you—or learn to deal—then school leadership isn't for you.

You can't not make decisions. You can't avoid some people being angry. The school as a whole is counting on you to make decisions. That's what leadership is: to decide where to go and, despite the difficulties, to move your school forward.

How This Book Works

Tough dilemmas get easier if you know how to navigate them. In this book, I've synthesized the latest research in cognitive science and expert decision making into a five-question framework. When you understand each question and how to apply it, you can use the questions to make better decisions for your school. Each question has a chapter to build your understanding that features true stories and examples. For instance, for the question "Where's the trade-off?" I examine how disciplinary decisions force school leaders to weigh competing values and interests. That's not because "Where's the trade-off?" is the only question that applies to discipline; you should also ask yourself the other four questions about major disciplinary decisions, or any of your big challenges! While the questions are easy to remember, the examples will help you understand the complexity each question raises. Each chapter closes with an opportunity for reflection to help you analyze your own values and decisions so you can grow.

Of course, not every decision needs to be a hard one. You'd be paralyzed if you followed a five-question process about whether to drink the expired cafeteria milk (don't) or take a turn in the dunk tank on Field Day (do). You'd be too slow if, when the fire alarm went off, you searched for this book, reviewed the five questions, and followed a careful process for how to respond. Instead, these five questions will serve you in two ways: when faced with an important, vexing decision, you'll have a path forward; and, by using this process, you'll build the habit of strategic decision making so that it becomes subconscious and automatic, even while the fire alarm is ringing.

For now, though, and throughout the book, my aim is to question what's subconscious and automatic. This is largely a book about not making assumptions; we need to recognize how limited our usual approaches are, and we need to move past typical habits so that we can improve our schools.

I am, however, making one big assumption: you care about kids, and you decided to become a school leader because you want the best for them. Your caring makes decisions harder, but it's also the reason for leadership. As crossing guard and in every other form of school leadership, your care provides the goal; now the question is how to get there. Make the path through the traffic; make paths for kids, and for your school, to succeed.

Know Yourself

As with any path, you should start this work from where you are! Reflect on your experience with tough decisions.

- What dilemmas are hardest for you—discipline, staffing, budget, curriculum, or some other area? What makes them hard?
- How do you make decisions currently? Do you use a formal or conscious process? If not, what are the informal or subconscious steps you usually take?
- What major decisions do you face now or have coming up? What makes them major? How will you approach them?
- What decision do you remember that you feel you got wrong? What parts of your process led you down the wrong path?
- What decision do you remember that you feel you got right? If it was difficult, what helped you move ahead?
- What decision do you remember that you just didn't make? Why did you avoid deciding? How did that work out?
- Why did you decide to read this book? How do you want it to affect your leadership path?

Question 1

What Am I Missing?

Nobel Prize winner Daniel Kahneman trained as a psychologist but won his fame (and Nobel) in the world of economics. He showed how irrational humans are—and how consistent, and therefore predictable, our errors are. He summarized the way we err with the acronym WYSIATI, for "What You See Is All There Is." That is, we make judgments using the information at our disposal, even if the right information is lacking—and we do so by convincing ourselves that we're seeing the complete truth.

That's abstract, obviously. Here's an example. One 2nd grade teacher runs the quintessential tight ship. Her bulletin boards are organized; her students line up quickly; she turns in all her paperwork on time. The other 2nd grade teacher is beloved by students and parents alike. Previous students return to give him hugs; his children run down the hall to greet him in the morning; the opening circle in his classroom resounds with happiness and song.

Which teacher is more likely to improve reading achievement?

The answer is that we have no idea. (Though you might have been tempted to guess, and you certainly have a bias for which teacher you prefer!) None of the information presented is about reading achievement. The scenario creates an intuitive problem, as Kahneman (2011) says, "When faced with a difficult question, we often answer an easier one instead, usually without noticing the substitution" (p. 12). In this case, we substitute either "Which teacher has strong classroom management?" or "Which teacher has great relationships?" for the real question of reading achievement.

To stop and reflect, to wonder whether we have enough information, takes time. Yet time is the most crucial resource for principals, and the scarcest. Lack of time leads you, predictably, to a particular kind of error in judgment. It's also covered by What You See Is All There Is: the belief that the inevitably small slices of school life you see are representative of school life as a whole. You see five minutes of class, and you believe you know what the teacher is like generally; you see a student misbehave, and you infer how constant a disruption she is.

Intellectually, you know that these inferences aren't usually accurate. But what we know intellectually, or consciously, has to fight with the judgments we make unconsciously. Those five minutes may have been among the worst (or best) of the year for that teacher, and when we're writing his evaluation that afternoon, we'd better understand that! If we don't, we fall victim to availability bias—when what's easy to think about (more available to our minds) seems more representative than it actually is. My favorite example of this isn't from schools; it's from home. Between you and your spouse or roommate, who does what percentage of the household chores? If we ask you and the other person, each of your answers for yourself will certainly add up to more than 100 percent. Even if you admit the other does more—say, you only do 40 percent—that person will most likely still estimate 80 percent. That's because you remember all the chores you do; cleaning toilets is pretty memorable! But it's harder to bring to mind the chores your spouse does.

The key challenge for school leaders is to know that our information is limited and to ask the first big question: "What am I missing?" Remember what Kahneman describes: without noticing, people often choose the easiest answer that comes to mind, even if it's to the wrong question. It's the "without noticing" that you can train yourself to avoid. Principals can't observe every minute of a teacher's practice or every instance of a student's behavior, and we can't know everything that could factor into every decision we make. But we can recognize our overactive tendency to believe that what we see is all there is—the mistaken assumption that the slices we *can* see are truly representative of those we can't.

THE WRONG PATH: THE DRUNK IN THE LIGHT

Walking home late at night, I saw a man, smelling of alcohol, scouring the ground under a streetlight. When I asked him what happened, he replied, "I lost my keys."

"Oh, you dropped them here?" I said.

"No," he said, motioning across toward the dark side of the street. "I dropped them over there, but it's easier to see here in the light."

This didn't happen to me, of course; it's an old story. But the equivalent happened to me many times—except I was the drunk, not the passerby. And I wasn't actually drunk—being drunk at school is a very foolish thing to do!—but I did make the same mistake: looking for answers where it was easy to look rather than where the answers actually were.

We do this when we analyze data, when we interview teachers, when we make a big deal of student work displays. We do it whenever we mistake what's *easier to see* for what

CONTINUED

we *actually want to know*: which multiple choice option a student chose for what they were really thinking; which teacher candidate is most poised at an interview table for which teacher will increase student learning; the quality of the student work displayed in the hallway for the work of the class as a whole.

Appearances do matter in education. But we can't just look at what is shiniest where there is light.

It's almost as foolish as being drunk at school.

What Does the Fox See?

Everyone predicts the future. Only some get it right. Business school professor Philip Tetlock ran multi-year forecasting tournaments to find what he calls "superforecasters"—those who accurately predicted outcomes like elections, revolutions, and stock market highs. Pundits and experts weren't always superforecasters. In fact, those with big ideas didn't do well in the forecasting tournaments. "They sought to squeeze complex problems into the preferred cause-effect templates," writes Tetlock & Gardner (2015), "and treated what did not fit as irrelevant distractions" (p. 68). Tetlock likens these One Big Idea thinkers to hedgehogs, who have one trick, one strategy, and use it to brazen their way through every challenge. They're impressively confident; one CNBC host, an economist known for predicting continual growth, wrote in July 2008 that "we are in a mental recession, not an actual recession" as the economy went into freefall. When you look at their results, these hedgehogs actually do worse than random guessers in the long run.

How can your predictions—that is, your decisions about what will make the future better—improve? The superforecasters didn't have one trick. Instead, "these experts gathered as much information from as many sources as they could. When thinking, they often shifted mental gears, sprinkling their speech with transition markers such as 'however,' 'but,' 'although,' and 'on the other hand.' They talked about possibilities and probabilities, not certainties. And while no one likes to say, 'I was wrong,' these experts more readily admitted it and changed their minds" (Tetlock & Gardner, 2015, p. 68). These open-minded thinkers are foxes; they adapt, draw back, regroup, switch paths, and try again. They know that their first idea isn't necessarily right. They are willing to look again, to reconsider. They know they can't see everything at first glance. And they're the ones who win.

"OK," I hope you're saying. "I get it. Now make me a fox." Just sprinkling your conversation with *however* or *although* won't be enough. You need actions that can help you see what you're missing.

Expand What You See

Making a good decision requires knowing the landscape well; to know where to go, you have to know where you are. You can better learn your landscape through regular practices that move you beyond your (often mistaken!) gut—practices that show you why what you thought you saw *isn't* all there is. Tools for doing so include surveys, focus groups, and stack audits.

How are teacher–student relationships? What locations in your school are hot spots for bullying? Did Back-to-School Night work for parents? You can guess; you can hear from the most outspoken stakeholders, who have important things to say but are usually not representative. Or you can **survey**. Free tools like Google Forms make it almost negligent not to survey whenever the opinion of a large group matters to the decisions you'll make. If you want to improve relationships, prevent bullying, or have a successful Back-to-School Night next year, why would you not survey? Design your own or use one of the commercially available surveys from groups like TNTP (to survey teacher attitudes), Panorama Education (for student surveys about teachers and school), or Making Caring Common (for school climate surveys). These come with a price but offer comparisons to other schools and easy tools for analysis.

Surveys do take time and effort, especially if you want a large number of representative responses. E-mailing parents a link, for instance, won't usually do it; you'll get a much better response rate if you place tables with computers by the exit. There are simpler ways. I once did a live poll by standing in the cafeteria with a sign scribbled, "Do you feel we're preparing you for college?" and handing out sticky notes and pens for students to write their answer as they walked by. The answers weren't complex, but I did learn a lot.

I am always surprised by how much school leaders merely, and even subconsciously, guess at what's going on with their staff members or students. You can ask them! **Focus groups** are even easier than surveys, and both children and adults love being asked to participate. They can be two hours or 20 minutes, and, while an accurate sampling (representative according to whatever is important for the questions at hand—demographics, achievement levels, or otherwise) is useful, your thinking will be expanded no matter what. You can even just stop a couple of people in the hallway to ask a question. One principal recently showed me her weekly staff bulletin and asked how I thought it could be improved. I had some ideas, I told her, but my main advice was that she should just ask three teachers what they thought. It would take three minutes, build three relationships, and gain her much more insight. The updated bulletin has more consistent sections, is formatted to be more readable on a phone, and begins with shout-outs so that teachers are excited to start reading. More importantly, the principal shed her reputation for go-it-alone isolation; teachers noticed that she asked, listened, and changed.

Some kinds of understanding aren't best gained just from asking people. How challenging is the homework we assign? Are we communicating efficiently with all-staff e-mails? Are Do Nows in the school a valuable use of time? You can ask around, but adding up opinions isn't the best way to get a global sense of quality. Instead, you can use a **stack audit**: put every example of something in a stack (including a metaphoric or digital stack), and go through that stack to determine patterns and overall impact. Collect every homework assignment or Do Now for a day. Collect every all-staff e-mail sent over a week. Use a stack audit, unlike a focus group, when you want a truly representative set of data. But they're not as good as focus groups at the *why*, at probing for the reasons behind the data: Why does all the homework consist of low-level practice? Why do so many people send such a large number of e-mails that are relevant to so few recipients? You can follow up stack audits with a focus group to find out; or sometimes, a focus group can inspire an inquiry through a stack audit. It depends on the questions you want to answer and the amount of time—five minutes from every staff member or an hour from five in particular?—the answers will take.

Once you've gathered information, the challenge is to keep it all in mind. Remember the availability bias: what's easy to think about (more available to our minds) seems more representative than it actually is. So a particularly well-articulated statement, or an unusual expression, will stick in your mind, but that doesn't mean that it's the one to listen to. One student who says something outlandish in a focus group makes for a great story but not for a great sense of the overall opinion in the group. Daniel Kahneman, the Nobel Prize winner who taught us about availability bias, also warns us about the **peak-end rule**: along with outliers, it's easier to remember the end of an experience than the rest of it. If you do classroom walk-throughs, for instance—a great form of stack audit—you should know that the last classrooms you saw, along with the best and worst, are much likelier to stick in your head than the earlier and more typical examples. Don't sit down after a walk-through and immediately write down, or even talk through with others, your conclusions. Expand what you see by taking notes or ratings along the way, then review them afterward before you analyze the whole picture. This is what's called a **memory prompt**: when you know about the peak-end rule, you can prompt yourself to remember the rest of what you've seen. Memory prompts enable you to see the whole landscape for your decision.

Expanding What You See About Race

Some things you miss aren't just because of availability bias. You miss them—I certainly miss them!—because of deeper, longer-lasting blind spots. These blind spots stem from our identities. When we accept and recognize that *who we are* limits our perspective, we can expand our vision, better understand our world, and make better decisions for our schools.

What am I missing? The *I* part is crucial, and one area where school leaders need to be especially self-conscious is race.

The teacher in my office is named Sergio, and he's exasperated with people (other teachers, even school leaders) getting it wrong. Sergio, with the *g* pronounced as English would pronounce *h*; and not Santiago, the name of another Latino man at the school. "And we don't even look alike!" he says. "You have no idea the number of microaggressions I am subject to on a daily basis at this school." I don't. But at least he's telling me.

Race screws up vision. It creates biases, stereotypes, and blindness. That the infinite variety of human skin colors can be divided into categories that have anything to do with intelligence, morality, or capability: what a crazy, incoherent, irrational idea!

But in America today, no matter the good intentions, not seeing race screws up vision more. Race matters. Race matters to our children, our families, our teachers. Serving our students here, now, means accounting for and fighting racism. We can't teach our students of color without accounting for racism, and we can't prepare white students for a better world without an anti-racist approach in the work we do. Race is a social construct and also real; we can't get past racism without seeing race. As educators, we believe in individual success and autonomy. We have to believe that each student is a unique and powerful individual. (If not, what are we doing?) But we also have to recognize that the ways we *want* to see the world are not the ways we actually see the world. Studies of implicit bias, led by Harvard professor Mahzarin Banaji, reveal that the majority of white people have more positive subconscious attitudes toward white people than toward black people, and even a third of black people have a similar preference for white people (Project Implicit, n.d.). This is hard to accept if we are believers in anti-racist fairness. But we must be conscious to combat our own unconscious.

Even if we are among the minority of people who do not have this implicit racial bias, we must constantly struggle against the bias faced by our students of color. It starts by preschool, where teachers are more likely to see black children as misbehaving even when doing the exact same behavior as white children (Gilliam, Maupin, Reyes, Accavitti, & Shic, 2016). We are primed by our society to expect bad behavior from black students and similarly primed to expect less of them academically. Confirmation bias—the psychological phenomenon where people more easily find evidence that confirms, rather than refutes, what we already believe—literally makes us more likely to see the faults in black students. While research is less advanced for the effect of implicit bias on other racial groups, our view of children is influenced by the (false) stereotypes we all hear about them—criminal Latino boys, studious Asian children, innocent white girls.

Individual psychology, and the effects of bias on those of us in schools, aren't the only reasons we need to be conscious of race. Race matters in our society. From segregated cities to racial profiling by police and ordinary passersby, to the massive black–white wealth gap, our inheritance of racism continues to structure the different lives we live. The history of race means that we are not starting from scratch. Our youngest schoolchildren arrive with their lives already shaped—not determined, shaped—by that history. As school leaders, we need to know this history and these structural realities. As scholar Richard Milner (2015) writes, "It is difficult to have substantive conversations about race regarding individual students and their parents and families without thinking deeply about the broader collective, societal systems that directly impact the individual" (p. 10). We cannot understand lived experience in America, especially Americans of color, without understanding racism.

Leaders of color know how to do this; they've had to see racism their whole lives. White school leaders, being white, are particularly susceptible to racist biases and failing to counteract them. Even when we want to not be racist, we tend not to have personal experience with racism, so it's harder for us to see. We are also the heirs to centuries of prejudice, and to biases we would rather not have. White principals need racial humility: to accept that we may not see manifestations of racism that really are there and that different perspectives, including those that disagree with or attack us, really are important. We need to see the points of view that tell us we are wrong, including those that tell us we are racist, as painful as it is.

If you are white, accept and expect that people of color think about and see race more than you do—and they're probably right. Race is active in your school, and people of color have had to be more conscious of race than you throughout their lives. Their sense for it is better, and in general, they want you to acknowledge its presence and how it operates at your school. I often think of what one African American colleague said: "I don't want you to be colorblind. Don't say you don't see race. I'm black, and my blackness is a huge part of who I am. If you don't see race, you don't see me."

The psychological research tells us that we all have limitations. White people like me can work to see beyond ours. We can't rely on being corrected by others, given the privilege of our position—it's an unfair burden for them. Instead, we need to educate ourselves. Whiteness has so dominated public discourse that we can be shocked to see the world from other perspectives—and transformed when we gain perspectives on people of color beyond stereotypes. These come from conversations, literature, music, TV shows, and movies in which we deliberately expose ourselves to the unfamiliar. We can shadow students for a day. We can read the memoirs and scholarship of educators of color. We can, and should, hire nonwhite people. We can fight this manifestation of our own racism to expand our leadership for our schools.

Expanding What You See Beyond Teaching Staff

When I became an assistant principal, my principal assigned me to supervise the custodial team. On her part, this was a mixture of perversity and genius. I was an English-teaching intellectual fresh from a stint in the school system's central office—a dorky bureaucrat. In all honesty, I didn't really know how to clean, much less how to tell other people to clean. My principal informed me that this assignment would be good for my professional growth.

I would understand, in a different way, what makes a school work and how to lead one.

The custodians felt remote to me. Some had been cleaning buildings since I was in elementary school. I had a master's degree; none of them had been to college. They were all black; I am white. They worked hours that started before anyone else, with one supervisor opening the building, or ended after everyone else, with another supervisor locking up. Like many of our teachers, I had moved to Washington, D.C., as an adult; they were all natives. Of course, we had common interests: I shared pictures of my son, and they shared pictures of their children and grandchildren. We were all happy when we ordered barbecue for lunch. But I was their boss, in training to be the big boss; their professional goals were mostly holding on to their good union jobs and looking for a better schedule and possibly a promotion to supervisor (which still involved cleaning a section of the building, just for better pay). To a great degree, I lived for my work. They worked to pay for life outside their work.

I can deal with, and enjoy, the differences among human beings. It was the differences that directly related to the work that I found frustrating. Middle school students leave trash around. (I wish they wouldn't, but they do.) After lunch especially, I walked the halls and found food wrappers, milk cartons, and illicit soda cans. I picked them up when I saw them, but I wanted the custodians to make an after-lunch building sweep part of their routine. It seemed straightforward to me—and anything but easy to them. They tried to explain their routines, which included a collective deep clean of the cafeteria after lunch. They had systems. But, I asked, why couldn't they take ten minutes and go to their building sections, pick up trash, and return to the cafeteria to deep clean? I talked to the supervisors, and I talked to the team. It still didn't happen. I just didn't get it. We agreed, at least, on that: I just didn't get it.

You might be familiar with the idea of **theory of mind**. It's a curious name for a straightforward understanding: that other people have minds of their own, with their own information, desires, and dreams. Even very small children have theory of mind. They know when their knowledge is different from another person's (which is why they find secrets so interesting); they know that they can be sad when somebody else is happy. But sometimes children, and even adults—especially principals—struggle with theory of mind. We don't always understand that others think differently from us or apply our own complexity to others' interiority to fully acknowledge their perspectives, hopes, or ideas. It's not always easy to make this particular kind of mental leap: that the way you think and what you know are different from, and not necessarily greater than, the way others think and what others know.

Like me, you were probably a teacher before you became a school leader. Though sometimes you strain to remember what it was like, you don't struggle with theory of mind when it comes to teachers. But custodians—or secretaries or counselors or speech therapists—can be baffling. It's not that they're unimportant. It's a cliché that the school secretary is the one who knows everything about the school, but it's a cliché because it's true. The front desk receptionist sets the tone for visitors and parents. School security guards transition students from their outside lives to their educational days. Counselors can prevent a suicide or uncover bullying. Custodians make the difference in whether a school is clean and well lit, and therefore feels orderly, or not. However, to acknowledge the importance of these nonteaching positions among school staff does not mean that you understand them. It doesn't even mean that you have a theory of mind for them.

At least, I didn't. I didn't get it. I couldn't understand why the custodians couldn't just change their ways as I wanted them to.

Every individual is an individual. But we are trained in common ways of thinking through our formal training, and especially through our work, our habits, our daily existence. A custodian sees the building differently than a security guard. A counselor sees a misbehaving child differently than a teacher. A principal's theory of mind needs to extend to all staff members, to understand that there are different ways of looking at the world of the school, with reasons and experience behind them. This understanding is a recognition of our own limitations. Theory of mind is not just a theory of other people's minds; it's acknowledging that our own minds are not all-encompassing or coterminal with truth.

For all the importance of other school staff, the purpose of the school is to teach. How do you maintain a focus on teaching without alienating nonteachers? The key is to strive to see through your other staff members' eyes. Staff members who aren't teachers don't see the school like teachers, and they certainly don't see the school the way you do. That's not because they are especially limited; you don't, and can't, see the school the way they do either! As Jody Heymann (2010), a business school professor, writes, "Companies need to establish ways to learn from their lowest-level employees, who have the most expertise on the ways in which much of the work at the company is done and could be improved" (p. 226). Your custodians think differently. It's likely that they think better about their work than you do.

That's what I learned, as an assistant principal, when I figured out how to talk to the custodian team. Or, more accurately, when I figured out how to *listen* to them! They explained how demoralizing it felt to clean the same areas of the building multiple times rather than once at the end of each day. They taught me how lonely cleaning could be; although sometimes they squabbled, they appreciated the brief period of teamwork as they cleaned the cafeteria together after lunch. They also felt that, after years of experimenting, they'd divided up the cafeteria work fairly: less squabbling! To pull adults away from their teamwork to pick up after litterbug kids not only was an affront but messed up a system that worked.

My perspective wasn't wrong—we did need to make the building look less trashy after lunch—but neither was theirs. We talked through it. We ended up with the custodial supervisor walking the building with students who had been caught littering. The other custodians grew by handling the cafeteria cleanup without the supervisor. The supervisor spent time with kids who needed to learn the impact of their actions, to understand the perspectives of the people who pushed the brooms. The kids grew; the supervisor, by getting some moments to mentor challenging students, did too. I still picked up trash in the hallways when I saw it. I still missed a lot of what they saw, but I was trying to learn.

Expand Your Possibilities

The custodians and I, when we were at an impasse, faced an either/ or choice. Either the building would be trashy after lunch, or the custodians would clean it up. We got past the impasse by creating an additional choice.

Having **multiple options** for a problem will always lead you to a better decision. One business study found that, in either/or decisions, the people who decide ultimately feel they'd failed more than half the time. But with multiple options, that feeling of failure drops to less than a third. As author Steven Johnson (2018) says, "If you find yourself mapping a 'whether or not' question, you're almost always better off turning it into a 'which one' question that gives you more available paths" (p. 67).

This is a form of "What am I missing?" that isn't about infor- mation gathering but instead possibility expansion. Like all of the aspects of "What am I missing?" it involves a form of mindfulness: to notice when you've given yourself an either/or and then to push your mind (or better yet, ask your colleagues) to come up with something else. It's applicable with students in trouble: to suspend or not? Maybe there's another possibility. It's applicable to purchase requests: to approve or not? It's applicable to curriculum choices, to master scheduling, to your own schedule. If it's important, it's worth considering multiple options. One way to make sure you're doing so is to write them down. If you have only two items on your paper (or whiteboard or Google doc), it's time to brainstorm more.

That's easier said than done, of course. How do you come up with more? Paradoxically, one approach is to imagine an obvious path is closed. If there were just no way to approve the purchase request—say, for a class set of graphing calculators—what would you do? Maybe a nearby school has devices you can share. Maybe students can get a free app on their phones. Maybe more creative paper-and-pencil strategies will actually help them learn more. That's not to say buying the calculators is the wrong option; it's just that you, and your staff, can think beyond it if one path were closed. Another way to expand options is to ask those who don't usually weigh in. Marginal views can see possibilities that others miss. To suspend or not? Try asking the worst-behaved student you know, or the most socially isolated, to suggest a different consequence. They might suggest an alternate in-school placement or a complex form of restitution or a restrictive behavior contract. They might suggest something not doable or unethical, like a dunce cap, or worse! They might have no good ideas. But they will think of things you haven't and thereby help you expand your own thinking.

School leadership is full of tough choices. Multiple options don't make it easier—using them is not a way out of tough choices. Rather, considering multiple options is another way to see the full landscape in front of you. You still have to choose a path, which will disappoint some and please others. But you might be able to make a path you didn't know was there.

Clarify Your Theory of Action

Your final challenge, to ensure you're not missing something when you look at your decision-making landscape, is to ensure that the path you choose actually leads where you want to go. For Dorothy and Toto, the yellow brick road actually does lead to the Emerald City. But too often, we lay down wishes rather than actual bricks; we think that, because we want a road to take us there, it actually will. This is **magical thinking**, without the ruby slippers: the belief that unrelated events have something to do with each other when in fact they are linked only by our wishes. Toddlers are masters of magical thinking; they really believe their stuffed animals can move in the night and that temper tantrums can make their parents "go away!" School leaders aren't prone to this kind of magical thinking. But we are prone to optimism—otherwise why would we be working in the circumstances we do?—which creates its own kind of magical-thinking blindness. We'll institute this program, announce this initiative, update this system, and the teachers will teach better, the students will learn better, the school will improve. If we put motivational signs on the walls, students will be better motivated. (Why?) If we give interim assessments, teachers will more successfully target instruction to student strengths and weaknesses. (How?) The point isn't that these are bad actions; it's that the logic is incomplete, and we are missing the crucial steps. We engage in magical thinking because we want things to work. We want good ideas to make a difference. But if we refuse to think hard about the internal logic of our plans, our good ideas will fail.

We can avoid this kind of magical thinking if we are explicit about our **theories of action**. Theories of action are if–then statements that make explicit the connection we see—or hope for—between what we do and the results we seek. If we put up motivational signs, then students will be better motivated; if we give interim assessments, then teachers will use targeted instruction. We make them explicit to see the missing links. Will the students read the motivational signs? Will they understand the message? If students read and understand a motivational message, do we actually believe they are then better motivated? Theories of action can raise more questions, questions about how we believe the world works: What model of student motivation are we using? Is it one where their motivation can be moved by synthesizing clever slogans? These are often hard, complicated questions. But they're necessary so we can better get to where we want to go.

Sometimes, theories of action can help us fill in blanks and change magical thinking to action steps. If we give (valid and reliable) interim assessments, then teachers have good assessments to evaluate student progress. If teachers have good assessments (and they know how to analyze those assessments), they can identify student strengths and weaknesses. If teachers can identify student strengths and weaknesses (and know a variety of instructional strategies, can manage a differentiated classroom, and have the time and mandate to do so), they will more successfully target instruction. This sounds a lot tougher than the magical-thinking version. But it's a lot more likely to avoid missing pieces. My school had a student-centered pedagogical approach, with lots of projects and choice. Our board of directors pushed me: "What is your theory of action for how this pedagogical approach improves outcomes for your lowest-performing kids?" We had answers about student engagement, about critical thinking, but as much as I wanted to, I couldn't come up with a theory of action for how our approach would improve their reading skills. That piece was missing, and we implemented an additional reading block featuring more teacher-led direct instruction. We couldn't call it student-centered pedagogy, but it centered on student needs, and the theory of action was now clear.

When you miss less, you have an unavoidably more complicated picture of the world. It's more accurate—because the world *is* complicated—but it can feel overwhelming. The false simplicity we had before built confidence. As Nobel Prize winner Kahneman (2011) explains, "The confidence that people experience is determined by the coherence of the story they manage to construct from available information. It is the consistency of the information that matters for a good story, not its completeness. Indeed, you will often find that knowing little makes it easier to fit everything you know into a coherent pattern" (p. 87). When you see what you were missing before, it's harder to bring coherence; when you see the complexity of the landscape in front of you, it's harder to make a path. We'll tackle that work in the next chapter. But for now, know that missing less can feel harder, but your vision will be a lot more accurate and a lot more likely to be fulfilled.

DON'T FORGET

Psychological research shows that human beings miss a lot of what goes on around them without realizing they're missing anything at all. When you gather information for decision making, you miss less if you humbly accept that you don't know it all. Look for ways to expand your thinking.

- Get outside your own head: use surveys, focus groups, and stack audits.
- Avoid the peak-end problem: use memory prompts to review information you gather.

CONTINUED

- Beware your own identity-based perspective. If you're white, accept that race is likely at play in ways you don't see. If you were a teacher, expect that nonteaching staff have their own ways of thinking that are valid too.
- Explore possibilities: expand your options beyond either/ or choices.
- Beware magical thinking: explicitly state your theory of action without skipping steps.

Know Yourself

Everyone has blind spots. Just like in a car, if you know where your blind spots are, you can be sure to check them! Reflect on your own practices.

- Do you regularly survey your staff, students, and other stakeholders?
- This week, have you asked for in-person feedback from staff members or other stakeholders? If so, are the people you asked for feedback the same people you always ask?
- This week, have you done a walk-through, stack audit, or other random sample of the work in your school?
- What is your racial identity? Do you regularly talk to people with other racial identities about how race affects your school?
- Were you a teacher? Do you regularly talk to staff members other than teachers—including lower-paid employees—about the school, their work, and how to improve both?
- Do you write down options for important decisions and make sure you have more than two?
- Do you explicitly state a theory of action for important initiatives and make others do so when presenting initiatives to you?
- When making judgments about your school, do you slow down and ask yourself, "What am I missing?"

QUESTION 2

WHAT'S ONE SMALL STEP?

The problem with schools is that there are so many problems. I was hired to consult at a high school that epitomized this—a school where just about everything was wrong. To be clear, the people weren't wrong: the students were typical teenagers, the teachers cared, the leadership team tried hard and believed in greatness. But when they came together, very little worked. Lessons went nowhere. Homework went undone. Tardiness was high, attendance was low, test scores were even lower. I arrived at a point of crisis. Students dropped out, and teachers quit midyear. Many students couldn't read, and many others didn't see the point. Fights and outright disruptions were rare, but that was due more to a cycle of disengagement than to any kind of positive culture.

The problems at this school were big. But a good leader can usually see big problems anywhere. What school doesn't have them? And when faced with those big problems, ambitious leaders look for big solutions. The best leaders, though, temper their ambition; they test solutions through small steps to prevent big errors and find pathways that work. Even at a school where almost nothing seems right, the greatest of journeys begins with a single step.

Remember the superforecasters, the thinkers with outstanding ability to predict the future? Their strategy to deal with the overwhelming nature of big problems is named after another Nobel Prize winner, this one in physics: Enrico Fermi, whose investigations in nuclear reactions helped lead to the atom bomb. (Don't blame him for the bomb, though nuclear explosions are a good example of relatively small steps leading to very big change!) Fermi was known for his ability to figure out hard questions outside physics. The classic Fermi question is "How many piano tuners are there in Chicago?" To **Fermi-ize** a question like this, as Tetlock and Gardner (2015) explain in *Superforecasting,* is to find the smaller, solvable problems in overwhelmingly complex challenges. At first glance, there is no way on earth to figure out how many piano tuners there are in Chicago! But you can . . .

- Know how many people there are in Chicago,
- Estimate how many people live in a house and what proportion of houses have pianos,
- Guess how often pianos have to be tuned and what the workload of a piano tuner might be,

. . . and come up with a decent estimate. A Nobel Prize winner, it turns out, doesn't always think bigger thoughts than the rest of us. The winning strategy can be to think smaller.

The superforecasters Fermi-ize questions about the future. Your job is to Fermi-ize the problems of your school. Start by asking yourself, "What's one small step?" It's OK if the problems are big; the task is to break them into tractable subproblems.

THE WRONG PATH: WHAT NOT TO DO WITH HARD PROBLEMS

As principal, starting around January 3, I had an easy answer to just about every tough question: we'll figure it out over the summer. Ah, summer. That magic time when I could wear short sleeves, read a bunch of books, maybe even take an online course, and my leadership team could hold hours-long meetings to really delve into the big problems and come out refreshed with similarly big answers.

Summer is indeed a wonderful time for educators. And hours-long meetings can be useful. (So can books, I hope!) But this approach had two major problems. First, it meant that problems we identified after January 3 simmered (or boiled) for half the year. Second, it meant that the solutions we identified during the summer were solutions that seemed right in an empty school building, with hours of luxurious reflection, rather than in the fast-paced, crowded world of real school.

The same approach, with the same downsides, is often taken by well-meaning leaders at all times of the year. Is attendance low? We'll create a committee! With weekly meetings! To review the data and read the research! To discuss initiatives. . . . We think that we can best deal with a problem by getting away from it, understanding it comprehensively, and laying out a well-considered, large-scale approach. Meanwhile, the kids still aren't coming to school, and at the end of the committee process, we have a comprehensive plan that doesn't move the needle.

The funny thing is, this approach that seems so carefully considered stems from an instinct of fear, which moves us away from action and, in fact, away from reality. It's safer to study than to act, so our lizard brains scuttle away to the committee meeting. A more *truly* thoughtful approach is actually to think a little less—but try a little more!

Whether it's the committee, the pile of books, or the in-depth summer planning, beware the delaying tactics that stem from the common instinct to stay in the safe zone of *figuring out* a problem and never quite move on to *doing something* about it. You'll learn more from trying things than from discussing them. You'll also have fewer hours-long meetings and more time, next summer, to go to the beach.

So how do we do it? At the school where I was hired to consult, for instance, where just about everything felt wrong, how did we break down these problems into tractable pieces? The trick is to find a piece of the big problem that we can try to fix, starting now. This isn't a root cause analysis, where we break down the problem to find the underlying cause. The question is not "Why do we have this problem?" but instead "What is one piece of the problem we can solve?" If attendance is bad, can we actually make contact with every parent of an absent student by 10:00 a.m.? If students are cutting class, can we block off, or put an adult's desk in, their favorite place to hang out? These don't address the root causes of truancy or class avoidance. They aren't cost-free. But they're something to do, and worth trying. Maybe they'll make things a little better. If not, we'll try something else.

This wouldn't be the right approach if we weren't focused on the actual big problems. If a school with serious class attendance issues focused its culture team on a schoolwide talent show, they'd be avoiding rather than attempting. As fun and culture-building as a talent show would be, it won't get students into class! Similarly, if we don't have a theory of change for how the small step could affect the big problem, we're haphazardly flailing instead of scientifically experimenting. Fermi-izing is about finding a step that you have reason to believe will get you closer to the answer.

To break down big problems, look for the observable. A general sense that culture is bad is hard to act on. When students are congregating during class time in the back hallway, you can see that, which means you can do something about it. Fermi-izing issues in a school requires isolating where and when those issues happen, finding a time and place that can then be intervened. Is a teacher's classroom management poor? If by November it's ten minutes past the bell without class really having started, and four students are asleep, six are looking at their cell phones, three have their hoods over their heads, two pairs are whispering, and the rest are vaguely waiting to learn, and the teacher's shoulders are slumped and she alternates between a murmur and a shout with nothing in between—well, you've seen this classroom, and you know how overwhelming it feels. But just by looking for specifics you've started to Fermi-ize. The teacher can greet students at the door with a ready-to-go Do Now. She can fix her body language or her tone of voice or enforce the cell phone policy. She can make sure there's work to do and positively narrate the students doing it. To observe for specifics is to find a place to start.

Design Experiments

Very young children know about starting small. They're close to the ground; it doesn't matter much if they fall down. As they grow, they grab a crayon and scribble for a moment: it's a train! They build with Lego, with puzzles, with Magna-Tiles, with sand. They love mazes; you run in, you get stuck, you start over and try again. That's part of the fun. That train isn't a train anymore; it's an airplane, an eagle, a phoenix. The path through the maze isn't where we thought it was. If we remain open-minded to what the small steps teach, we can surprise ourselves and learn.

One semiformal process for such experimentation is called **design thinking**. I learned about design thinking through School Retool, a professional development program run by the design firm IDEO and the d.school at Stanford. (Yes, the d.school is what it's called. They're designers. They're artsy!) School Retool calls its version of design thinking the **hack mindset**, with three key ingredients:

- Start small: What's a first step toward your aspiration?
- Bias to action: What's one thing you can do today?
- Fail forward: How can you learn from tries that don't fully succeed?

In other words, the hack mindset is about doing small things quickly and learning from them to make headway on big challenges. It accepts imperfection; that's why the actions are called *hacks* and not solutions.

It's worth acknowledging that the hack mindset is hard for school leaders. We are responsible for the growth and the lives of young people. We have to do big things every day; we can't allow ourselves to just hack around, much less to fail (forward, or at all). We're working with children, not chairs or apps. We don't do clicks. We do learning. You want us to hack . . . humans?

Well, not when you're sure what works. But honestly, there are a lot of times when you're not sure. It's these times that experiments can help. It's better to be wrong with a small step, and learn you're wrong now, than to be big-league wrong and find out later!

Design experiments are worthwhile when school leaders see the need to change, to innovate, or to fix. Online marketers use **A/B testing** when they send two different versions of an e-mail, or show two different possibilities of a home page, to possible customers. The version that gets more clicks is the one they go with. And sometimes school leaders actually do want clicks: Are parents more likely to follow the "sign up to volunteer!" link if it's at the beginning or the end of the weekly newsletter? A/B testing is also useful for other kinds of marketing we do: Do more students come to tryouts for the school play if they're reminded on loudspeaker announcements or through hallway signs? But marketing isn't just advertisement; it's any time a school tries to get someone to do something. And it's worth A/B testing our strategies throughout. The first question in a job interview is marketing: What question best sets the tone for the new teachers you want? Arranging physical space is marketing: Do more students take fruit if it's placed at the beginning or end of the cafeteria line? Part of teaching is marketing too, selling the educational process itself: What Do Now or warm-up at the beginning of class best settles and engages the students? Trying a couple of options and figuring out how to track results is extra work. But if we want to *succeed* rather than just to muddle through, testing our ideas is worth it.

Small Steps, Big Changes

That first step takes bravery, but it's not nearly as scary as the consequences of standing still for too long. Designing experiments to help you determine your own first, small steps toward solutions might seem challenging, but if you look around your school for opportunities to test out new ideas, you'll be surprised at how many you'll find. As principal, I found the hack mindset and A/B testing useful for decision making across a number of different challenges my school faced, from school culture to curriculum to scheduling.

Using the Hack Mindset to Improve School Culture

Even the biggest, least specific, most important areas of school life are movable by the hack mindset. Take culture—one word for the common problem of the school I described at the beginning of this chapter. Culture is often defined as common attitudes, unspoken assumptions, the implicitly understood folkways of a group: in other words, what underlies behavior rather than any specific practices. But the behaviors that comprise culture can be seen, and, indeed, *must* be seen to be diagnosed or Fermi-ized. What about fixing culture? Again, advice to change culture often starts with a visioning process or collaboratively rewriting the school mission. That's the opposite of one small step; it's grand and time-consuming. And if it doesn't work, you won't know and won't be able to try again for a long, long time!

Instead, aim to *hack* culture with small, quickly doable steps that align. What makes culture? From one point of view, it's what is unspoken and implicitly understood. From another, it's the visible elements that signal how things are. Change them and you can change the culture. A song plays as students enter the building. A balloon animal hangs in the middle of the hallway. The teachers on cafeteria duty coordinate to wear red clown noses. None of these will be transformative, but together they signal levity and take small steps toward—if that's what you're going for—a more playful, joyous culture.

It's not that vision isn't important. Small steps only matter if they align with a vision. But the vision is actually the easy part. You already know your vision, even if not yet articulately; you could write it down in the margin of this page. And yes, you could word-smith it by committee, argue over adjectives with stakeholders, and have meeting after meeting to measure the right metaphor, but the vision you have right now, whether formally or informally, is just fine. The hard part (and the true disagreement) will come in the implementation. Spend your time and energy there, thinking about and trying out improvements.

There's no cultural vision in the world that doesn't include a caring, friendly community. (The stated vision might not include those words, but that's not the point.) There's also no school in the world that is as caring and friendly as it could or should be! How about a mix-it-up day, in which cafeteria seats or recess areas are assigned rather than chosen, and students are given conversation prompts or new games with which to meet new people? That won't achieve the vision, but it's a step, and one that can be repeated, evolved, and learned from. Speaking of lunch, how about asking grandparents to volunteer their presence during students' least structured times? This practice, which I picked up visiting an elementary school, provides additional eyes, role models, and community connections. Even one grandparent can make a difference. It's a small step toward a caring, friendly community. Speaking of cross-age connection, how about a buddy program where older students mentor younger students? That's a big task, but you can start small with just a couple of students, each mentor pair a step toward a grand vision.

The advantage of small cultural steps is that they assuage the natural human fear of change and the universal educator fear of a longer to-do list. Grand cultural plans can overwhelm. But one mix-it-up day, a few grandparents, a couple of peer mentors—these don't sound like too much to handle. If they work, they're easy to build on: we know how to plan another mix-it-up day; grandparents bring in other grandparents; peer mentors share excitement with friends who want in on the action. One small step can create a positive cascade.

Small cultural steps work with adults too. If you want a more collegial teacher culture, you can go crazy with structures and committees. You can also change the seating arrangement for faculty meetings from rows to small groups and, instead of making endless announcements, ask teachers to solve one problem together. When you buy coffee and donuts for a treat, you can put it in the new teacher's classroom (with permission) so that everyone who wants the caffeine and sugar ends up going to say hi. I've seen a couch in the staff lounge become a powerful relationship builder; people want to sit where it's comfortable, which means they sit next to each other, which means they get to talking. Highlighting one teacher's practice every week in your staff e-mail is quick and easy; it also spreads good pedagogy, signifies a focus on instruction, and suggests that excellence will be recognized. As with students, a small step doesn't change culture, but a lot of small steps can. You have to start somewhere, and it's best to get going.

Remember, if you don't have a theory of change for how the small step could affect the big problem, you're haphazardly flailing instead of scientifically experimenting. This is reverse-engineered

Fermi-izing: a narrative of how the small steps, over time, can add up. Vision isn't a small step, but it should be where the small steps take you; it's where you're going. What is the grandparents' presence supposed to do, and how will you know if it's doing it? What big problem is the couch in the teacher's lounge supposed to help with (not to solve; a couch alone has never solved a big problem!), and how will you know if it's helping? You can, and should, articulate why you're taking these small steps—especially to adults.

- "The coffee is in the new teacher's classroom so she can meet more people."
- "The couch is in the staff lounge so that teachers can sit and chat."
- "I'm adding a 'teacher practice of the week' to the staff e-mail to spread good ideas and show our focus on instruction."

All of these articulate the vision and connect it to a small step. They also clarify how you'll judge those steps. Do behavior incidents go down when the grandparents show up? Does the new teacher feel less isolated? Are people actually sitting on the couch, and do you ever see them in pairs you find surprising? Are the "teacher practices of the week" spreading beyond the original classroom? In other words, are those small steps taking you somewhere big, and if not, what else can you try?

Using the Hack Mindset to Improve Curriculum

If culture takes the prize for the biggest, hardest-to-grasp avenue for school improvement, curriculum has to be the runner-up. In proper perspective, the curriculum is everything the school teaches, from how to solve an equation to how to be a human being. Of course, we don't think of curriculum that way—it's impossible! It's too big! It's too much! Just the formal curriculum, such as the math textbooks we use or our social studies sequence, seems big enough. That's why changes to them are usually such big deals: extensive, sometimes multiyear processes involving committees, outside experts, board votes, and *lots* of money. Curriculum changes get this much front-end process because they're important but also because it seems too hard to know what we really care about: do they work?

The District of Columbia Public Schools system created a full curriculum but was still plagued by widely varied expectations among its incredibly diverse schools. It then took a different route. It created individual lessons, called Cornerstones, as a small (but ever-expanding) number of real-world-relevant, standards-aligned, student-centered activities for particular grades and subjects. Stringing bead bracelets to model addition and subtraction in 1st grade math, designing windmills in 4th grade science, delivering a TED talk in 8th grade English: these were small steps to showing teachers and students what was possible. And part of why they worked was that their small size makes the vision viewable. As Brian Pick, who led the Cornerstones effort, told me, "We had trained for years on 'inquiry-based math problems' but didn't see much uptake in the classroom until the math Cornerstones were introduced. Concrete. Bite-sized. Practical. Just in time training. Tools in place. And part of the larger math unit." The individual lessons gave teachers instructional models they could use in future units, techniques that fit into the larger inquiry-based vision. This is Fermi-izing an overwhelming problem: How do you get a whole district of teachers to lead inquiry-based math? It turns out that small steps provide a better path.

A single lesson, assignment, or unit can show what's possible. The key is to make it both doable and able to be followed up; a one-time activity that can never be repeated isn't actually a small step to a bigger vision. An international trip, or a week in which classes are canceled and everyone does an enormous project, can be a great experience for students. But taking the next step—that is, doing something similar again but bigger—isn't feasible. A second international trip? Cancel classes forever? Finding one small step isn't just about finding something small. It's about knowing where you want to go and moving in the right direction.

Among the most straightforward places for experimentation are the targeted curricula we call interventions. Whether known as Tier 2 or 3, support classes, or remediation, these exist because what we typically do doesn't work. And while evidence-based interventions exist and are important to find, the need to match them to a particular context—your school, a group of students in need, or this particular student right here—means that it's absurd not to proceed by small steps.

And yet too many leaders want a program of interventions, a system of interventions, or a suite. Companies and organizations selling interventions try to force this: Invest many thousands of dollars in our comprehensive approach! Buy the package! This research-based intervention only works if implemented with fidelity!

That last sentence is often true. But small steps don't have to mean they are piecemeal or subtractive. And they don't have to mean—and shouldn't mean—cartwheeling from program to program without the time or expertise it takes for any given intervention to actually work.

Instead, small steps for interventions are about scale. Rather than rolling out a new Response to Intervention (RTI) structure to the whole school, try it first with a single grade level. I did the opposite with a software program that promised to ease our RTI process. We did the first training for the whole school and only then found out that the software couldn't talk to our student information system software. After months of struggle, we abandoned it and got some of our money back. We couldn't get back the time and frustration, though.

Rather than placing all struggling readers in a support class, see how it goes with a few. Insist that salespeople let you trial: Is the software compatible with the computers you have? Does the timing work with your schedule needs? What can you learn from communicating the intervention to a few parents first, before rolling it out more broadly? Remember the first two ingredients of the hack mindset: start small and have a bias to action. But also remember the reason for the third ingredient, fail forward: a lot of things won't work, but if we find that out quickly, we can learn from failure at much lower cost.

The pressures that make us resist experimentation—these are students' lives, and they matter—can't keep us from experimenting, not if we want to improve. But we have to know what improvement means and to have explicit clarity about where we want to be. If we do, small steps can be the best way to get there.

Taking Small Steps on Master Schedules with A/B Tests

"The master schedule drives everything." If you've ever led a high school, you've heard that phrase. But even in middle and elementary schools, the master schedule structures the rhythms, the transitions, and even the learning of the day. When is recess? When are specials? Is the math block or the reading block first? Scheduling drives everything because so much of school is about avoiding chaos. When there are hundreds or thousands of children in a single building, vastly outnumbering the adults, especially by high school, when those children move from place to place independently, the schedule provides assurance that we have a plan, that we are in control. A principal I've worked with doesn't start her day with worries about testing next week, graduation next month, or hiring for next year; instead, she's most anxious to finalize the master schedule. It drives everything. And it also acts as a seal of good housekeeping: a place for everything and everything in its place.

Scheduling doesn't seem susceptible to small steps. It's called the *master* schedule for a reason. What could be bigger, less friendly to experimentation? That's where A/B testing comes in. Whiteboards and spreadsheets can tell you whether a new schedule will work mathematically. A test can show you how it works with those hundreds of bodies moving through space.

After I left, the school where I was principal considered moving from a traditional schedule to a block schedule. It's a combined middle and high school, and we'd thought about block scheduling before but never made the math work. Collaboratively, and with genius work by the master scheduler, a split middle/high schedule—in one building, with shared classrooms—was created. But as the middle school principal, Maya Stewart, told me, "Everyone sitting at the table could not actually see what we wanted to happen unless we tried it." They decided to pilot a single day of the new schedule in March.

"We got to see what it would actually feel like," Maya explained. "High schoolers got to transition without 6th graders running through their legs." The split schedule meant that the school didn't feel as if it were exploding every 55 minutes. That's what the whiteboard and spreadsheet predicted, but experiencing it is different. The school could see that many teachers' schedules wouldn't work with a split schedule; the calculations had predicted some holes that were filled in advance, but students still arrived at rooms with no teacher, and two classes expected to use the same room. Reality always works differently than predicted.

For school leaders, **pilots** are one way to figure out "What am I missing?" Like A/B testing, they realistically gauge audience reaction. At Maya's school, stakeholder surveys about schedule options had already happened before the pilot—and helped inform the design of the pilot—but they surveyed teachers and students at the end of the pilot day too. Remember that A/B testing is about marketing, and any time a school tries to get stakeholders to do something—like get to class safely and on time—that's a form of marketing. In this case, the A in the A/B test was the current schedule; the question was "How did the stakeholders react to B?" All of this was a lot of work. "It took so much brainpower," said Maya. "I wonder where else my spirit should have been." But it took less work than fixing a master schedule in September. "Pilots are great," Maya concluded. "I'm happy to work at a place where, if we need to test it out, we do."

If a new master schedule for a 1,000-student school can be tested one day in March before implementation in a new year, what can you try?

What Assessing Progress Does—and Doesn't

I want to refute one possible misimpression about small steps. It's the idea that assessment counts.

Information gathering to know what you're missing matters, of course. But diagnosis isn't the same as action. You aren't taking steps to make change until you are *taking steps to make change*. If you want to take small steps—and you should—those steps need to represent steps toward a solution, not toward an analysis.

On the other hand, if you are taking small steps—an action toward improvement—it's crucial not to forget that experiments exist for learning. Assessment isn't a small step, but if you don't plan to assess your small steps, you're missing the point. Like Maya with the schedule pilot, designing assessment as part of the experiment will help you learn. You can do so through a detailed theory of action: Fermi-izing how what you're trying will lead to what you want. If you plot out the steps, then at each small step you can see if you're heading in the right direction. The path is a hypothesis. The point is to test it.

After all, your experiment likely won't be perfect. There will be both successful and flailing aspects. (Hopefully no total disasters; that's why you take *small* steps!) If you knew what would work, you wouldn't be experimenting. And there are downsides to experiments: people are doing things for the first time. They're in unfamiliar territory, where errors happen more than usual. Expect a little chaos. Expect lower quality. The learning is worth it. As educators, we know discomfort is often where the learning happens.

DON'T FORGET

Too often, our impulse is to figure out, through an extended process, how to solve everything at once. Instead, we should look for small steps we can take to move us quickly in the right direction—or at least, help us learn from small mistakes. How can we move forward?

- Break down overwhelming problems into bite-size subproblems. This process, called Fermi-izing, helps you make educated guesses about where to take action.
- Design thinking and the hack mindset give you permission to accept imperfection through experimentation. If you don't know what will work, try *something*.
- Investigate multiple options through A/B testing. It's a marketing strategy applicable anytime you want stakeholders to say yes to an aspect of your school.
- You can take small steps to solve big problems, including culture, curriculum and grading, student interventions, and scheduling. These can be small-scale or temporary pilots of big changes to come, as long as they're designed so you can learn from them.
- Be sure to plan how to assess your small steps. Just don't mistake assessment for action!

KNOW YOURSELF

Small steps don't come naturally to ambitious leaders. We get into this work because we want to make a big difference at a big scale. Reflect on your own impulses.

- When you think about the big challenges at your school, how often do you feel they are too big to tackle? How often do you break those big challenges down into smaller pieces?
- How much certainty or support do you need before you can take action?
- When you introduce a new initiative, do you see it as a learning opportunity whether or not it works? Do you describe it to others that way?
- How often do you pilot several ways of doing something before deciding to go all in on one?
- Do you build in a plan for assessment when you try something new at your school?
- What big vision do you have for your school? What will, concretely, look different if that big vision is achieved? Can you make that look different (even if the rest of the vision isn't achieved) *right now*?
- Is there a small step you can take tomorrow on a big challenge at your school? How about another small step next week?

WHERE'S THE TRADE-OFF?

Schools are, inherently, places of optimism and hope. We look at children and see the adults they could become; and we wouldn't be here, with the fluorescent lights and the cafeteria food and the tween-boy body odor, if we couldn't see a better future. But optimism shouldn't prevent us from seeing that our decisions come with trade-offs. Everything can't be done in the ways all our staff members, parents, and students want; if everyone could be happy, school leaders' jobs would be a lot easier!

The ability to see trade-offs is key, and it distinguishes the principal from other members of the school community. A hard fact of life for principals is that their staff members don't tend to acknowledge trade-offs. Teachers want smaller classes, period. The special education coordinator wants an aide in the support classroom (and so does the athletic director in the gym). Do faculty want the paid version of the math software, an additional planning period, a summer stipend, a release from lunch duty? If you ask them, yes. Yes, of course they do.

They're not doing anything wrong. Teachers and other faculty members *should* argue for what they want. It's not that they don't like to acknowledge trade-offs. It's that they don't *need* to. Teachers see the big picture in their classroom, and good teachers know their students' individual needs—one student needs to learn phonics, another needs to learn poetic devices, a third needs to throw out her chewing gum—plus the overall mood and long-term goals of the class. But they don't have to see the big picture of the whole *school*. Trade-offs aren't their job; they're the principal's.

This is obvious when the time of year for budgeting rolls around. But first-rate principals train themselves to see trade-offs all year long, even when a budget spreadsheet doesn't highlight the tensions or display a negative sign when we go wrong. Trade-offs in time and attention are actually the most important to see because their effects are so powerful yet so delayed. An English teacher wants kids to enter an essay contest; a special education teacher wants to open his classroom for early morning tutoring; a first-year teacher wants to coach varsity soccer. These are all good things, beautiful even, instincts to be applauded. It's the principal's job to think about what might suffer.

In many instances, the trade-off comes down to the individual needs versus the bigger picture or the larger policy. An assistant principal wants to meet every morning with a 7th grader who will benefit from some mentorship, but if that assistant principal isn't outside for arrival, what does that do to the start of the school day? If we create an intensive reading class for four students with one teacher, how does that change class size for the rest of the school? If we let an overwhelmed teacher take some extra leave, what precedent are we setting, and does it affect overall morale? A principal's inability, or refusal, to see the trade-offs is a recipe for resentment, inequity, and failure.

Most principals once were teachers, and they need to move past the limited view that is acceptable for teachers but catastrophic for principals. If they don't, the results are factionalism and resentment among staff, blind spots for the leader, lack of progress on the big issues, and terrible surprises when the consequences of limitations become clear. I worked with one school leader who led a science lunch club. She'd been a science teacher, and students wanted a science club; nobody else was available to lead it. But every teacher outside the science department resented the time and attention she gave the science club, and they scrutinized— unfairly but predictably!—every dollar and every special event the science club got. Students not in the science club felt alienated when they saw, even in casual ways, the relationships their peers had with the principal. And when interscholastic science competitions arose, the principal had to dedicate large amounts of time to them while giving science club parents hours of access that no other parents received. The other parents noticed and gossiped and complained. Her laudable intentions meant a small positive impact and a lot of grief.

The principal who fails to see the big picture inevitably fails his or her school. The principal's key responsibility, the reason the position exists, isn't to evaluate teachers, to mollify parents, or to manage bus schedules; it's to make hard decisions with the big picture in mind. Successful school leaders train themselves to look and ask, "Where's the trade-off?"

THE WRONG PATH: WE'LL DO IT BETTER HERE

There's a conversation elementary school teachers have with certain students on a regular basis. It's a certain type of student: the smart-aleck ones, those who try to get away with it, those lovable, big-for-their-britches button-pushers whose favorite mode of intellectual creativity is attempted rule evasion. The teachers—I can hear them now—stifle their grins, cock a fierce eyebrow, and say, in their no-nonsense voice, "You're special. But you're not *that* special."

Try reading the following paragraph in that same voice.

Your teachers are kind, expert, and determined. Your students are extraordinary and full of potential. Your community is strong, and your parents are caring. Your school is a truly special place. But it isn't *that* special.

Just like the mischievous rule tester needs to understand that the rules apply to him too, your school is subject to the same challenges and problems as other schools. If you assume that things will go better just *because* . . . well, they won't. It's very, very hard for a school to be an outlier. The teachers at the other schools, after all, are also kind, expert, and determined. The students at the other schools are also fabulous and full of potential, and their parents care just as much as the parents at your school. You can make your community strong—or stronger!—but magical thinking won't make it so.

The best leaders believe in their people and their place, but that belief becomes fantasy when you think the rules don't apply to you. Other schools have had to make trade-offs, and you will make your own trade-offs too. Catch yourself before you start to think, "If other places have low scores or high turnover or bad discipline, it must be because they're screwing up. We'll do it better here."

Not with that kind of thinking, you won't.

Avoid Overoptimism and Recognize Trade-Offs

I don't mean to be too tough on the science club principal, or on any principal. School leadership is hard. Schools are challenging places to lead—and impossible places to get right! Paradoxically, recognizing that hard truth can make the job easier because it allows us to accept the inevitability of trade-offs. There's often no right answer, no way to do things that will satisfy everyone and achieve everything we want. That recognition can help us see more clearly where responsibility lies. Seeing the issues *we're* having in the context of the challenges *everyone's* having can prevent us from misidentifying our challenges as the fault of a particular person or approach. When we know which problems are the fundamental problems of school, we can tell which are, by contrast, *our* problems in *our* school.

Sometimes, as with budgets, the trade-off is a matter of arithmetic: the bottom line shows that you can't have everything, and anyone can see that. But often—and this is why "Where's the trade-off?" is a question that separates outstanding school leaders from well-meaning but less effective ones—the trade-offs are harder to spot because they are a matter of prediction, not arithmetic. The trade-off doesn't show up on the bottom line; it's in the future. Cognitive scientists have lessons for school leaders on how to do prediction well. One, from Gary Klein in his book *Streetlights and Shadows* (2009), is taken from chess players who use a **mental simulation strategy** to compare important complex options. They "conduct mental simulations of each one of the promising moves, imagining how the option would play out deeper and deeper into the future. Then they take stock of their mental and emotional reactions to what they see in this mental review" (p. 96). If I do this, what happens next? What then? After that? How do others respond? How do I respond to their response? And so on, till I have a vision of where the game will stand in a future moment. Now how do I judge, and how do I feel about, that moment that will happen downstream?

The mental simulation strategy helps us see down the road and, especially, helps us see that our moves don't only follow our own trajectory: they provoke responses in others, to which we'll then have to respond. The world doesn't act the way we want it to! But we can still be overoptimistic when playing out this mental game. Klein (2009) proposes another strategy to avoid overoptimism, which he calls a **premortem**. He asks people to pretend they see, in a crystal ball, that in a few weeks or months their new venture will fail. What caused the failure? What didn't work? The premortem forces us to identify risks and downsides—the trade-offs that can kill the positive outcomes we'd otherwise focus on. That should be productive, not depressing. As Klein says, "We can't expect to fix all the flaws, but we can prepare ourselves and our teams by anticipating some of the problems" (p. 63).

This is hard because, when it comes to our own ideas, we just love to put on rose-colored glasses. Daniel Kahneman (2011) explains predictive failures with the **planning fallacy**, in which we imagine the best-case scenario for our plans rather than their most realistic outcomes. If we adopt this new curriculum, it's so tempting to trace a path to skyrocketing student achievement: teachers will love the curriculum, the books will come in on time, they'll be used with fidelity, the students will engage at such high levels, and just wait for the test scores. We can avoid the planning fallacy with what Kahneman calls the **outside view**, where we improve our predictions looking at what's happened with similar efforts in other cases. What happened when other schools or districts adopted this same curriculum? Did everything go perfectly? What happened when we adopted other curricula in the past? If we take the outside view, things don't look so rosy.

New schools are particularly susceptible to the planning fallacy and therefore in need of the outside view. When I joined a new middle school as the founding principal, I asked my supervisor which staff members she foresaw dealing well with fights and similar discipline problems. She had spent time at feeder elementary schools, and she told me, "These kids are coming from schools with great cultures. We won't have a lot of discipline issues." These kids *were* coming from schools with great cultures, but the outside view—that is, knowledge of how middle schools generally are—told me that we were sure to have a *lot* of discipline issues! I created a rotation of staff members to be on discipline duty. Midway through the first year, we hired a dedicated discipline specialist; the trade-off with other staff members' time meant that we were better off, like most schools, with someone who could focus exclusively on behavior. (Another win for the outside view!)

Similarly, I've worked with high schools that start with a college-for-all mission and mindset. I admire and support their high expectations and equity-driven ambitions. But there's almost no public school in the country that sends all of its students to college—certainly not open-enrollment public schools serving high-poverty populations. If the schools' leaders care about all of their students' futures, they need to make sure that even those who don't go to college have a solid post-graduation plan. With the outside view, they can avoid getting caught up in their hopes for a best-case scenario and see their own situation as like others'.

This acknowledgment is hard and in itself a trade-off: we live and work in the real world, and we need realism to balance optimism. When we acknowledge negative possibilities and trade-offs, we can plan to face them better and plan to avoid them. We can use the mental simulation, premortem, and outside view strategies to make sense of the most vexing decisions principals have to make.

Trade-Offs Toward Results

While trade-offs can be tricky, trying to do it all might keep you stalled. Using mental simulations, premortems, and outside view strategies will help you weigh your options and make the necessary shifts to get your school unstuck. At my school, these strategies helped me make better decisions in some of the most sensitive areas of our work, including discipline, data, evaluation, and time management.

Using Mental Simulations in Discipline

The trade-offs of school discipline are reflected in a hilariously apt first-person article titled "I'm Here for Restorative Justice Practices Until Your Son Punches My Daughter at School" (Stewart, 2018). Everyone's interests aren't the same, and win-wins aren't always possible. We're here for kids, of course, but discipline problems—whether between students or with persistently disruptive students—force us to question exactly which kids.

The hardest decisions I ever had to make were about expulsions. I tried to figure out what I was missing, to make sure I had all the details and different perspectives about incidents and histories. But I was always left with two fundamental questions: What will happen to this student if I put him out, and what will happen to the rest of the students if I let him stay? These are both unanswerable questions—as many thousands of students as I'd known, even as well as I knew this particular student, I didn't know the future. I had to go on the information I did have.

My lack of knowledge, my recognition that these questions were unanswerable, didn't prevent me from having to answer them. The trade-offs were my job! This is where the **mental simulation** strategy comes in. I did have information, after all. I had a good idea of where the student might go if expelled. I knew his family supports. On the flip side, I knew what he was like at school; I knew how he related to other kids, and they to him; I had a sense (and if I asked, "What am I missing?" could get more) of what those kids thought should happen. I could play the simulation forward. My predictions could be conscious and considered rather than implicit.

Even in a conscious mental simulation, though, my hopes for this student could make me overoptimistic about whichever decision I made. If expelled, I could imagine he would have a wake-up call; his parents would change their approach; he would find a new school and make a fresh start. That all sounds nice and plausible. If not expelled, I could imagine the near miss would also be a wake-up call; we would support him, his friends would rally around him, and students he'd harmed would come to see he could change. That also sounds nice and plausible.

But a premortem could help me better imagine where each path could go wrong. If he were expelled and ended up dropping out—not the result I wanted—what path would he take to that point? (And how could I prevent that?) If not expelled and he continued to cause serious harm at my school, what opportunities would I have missed? And could I take the outside view—what has happened to other students who have been expelled, or who haven't? This child was unique, all children are, but if I didn't think he would be similar to the statistics of similar cases, I needed to think hard about why not.

None of these thinking strategies could make the decision for me. But I would have a better, more thoughtful decision for putting in that work.

The decision was mine to make, but, as usual, it wasn't like I could go hide in the woods for a few days to make it. In addition to the usual business of running a school, parents and teachers and counselors who knew about the situation were contacting me to tell me what they thought should happen. And, of course, they didn't all think the same! Discipline is a matter of values—values for child-rearing, children speaking up versus children obeying, parents as coaches versus parents as commanders, compromising with others versus sticking up for yourself—and morality—what we consider morally bad and how bad. I was in a room of school leaders where we realized we had a profound disagreement on who had done something worse: the girl who hit a boy or the boy who spit on her. Some of the adults saw the punch as more violent. Some found the body fluid more violating. Not everyone has the same values.

Stances on disciplinary decisions can be influenced by personal interest; I've spoken to many parents who want other people's children suspended but never their own! Yet larger cultural and societal tensions are at work as well. In the room I was in, the school leaders who saw the punch as worse were white; those who saw the spit as worse were black. Those of us who are white learned, that day, about the special harm many black people feel in being spit on. The practical way to decide on disciplinary consequences for this incident meant figuring out how to balance, or trade off, those views.

Creating a policy is one approach. In the abstract realm of policy, we can calmly direct ourselves beyond moments of passion; the wisdom of policy is supposed to be the antidote to "I'm here for restorative justice until your son punches my daughter at school!" Policy means to clarify, to remove the haze when we see red. The problem, when it comes to discipline, is that policy inevitably obscures our vision of the people at the center of the trade-off, and it invariably misses the particulars of any given disciplinary situation. As Richard Milner (2015) writes in *Rac(e)ing to Class: Confronting Poverty and Race in Schools and Classrooms*, administrators "have the power to suspend or expel students based on (1) their *interpretation* of the misbehavior described by the teachers and (2) their *interpretation* of rules and policy violation" (p. 123). Nothing is as clear-cut as a policy description imagines it. My son's elementary school handbook list of Tier 3 behaviors includes "causing or about to cause significant harm to self or others," "violence toward staff," and "hate speech." There's a lot of—very necessary—room for interpretation there, even in

the more straightforward categories of weapon and drug posses-
sion. Is a knife left in a backpack from a Boy Scout camping trip a
weapon? Is cough syrup, brought to school with the intent of getting high on it, a drug? If you offer somebody else a sip of it, is that
distribution of alcohol? In the messy realm of real-life discipline,
policy often can't guide.

Policy does serve one important function: it gives us a basis outside of emotion for decisions. In discipline, too often, the decisive
human element is *fear*. And fear, in America, is deeply embedded
in racism. As Milner (2015) writes, "students of color—particularly
black and brown students—and those from lower socioeconomic
backgrounds are disproportionately punished and receive harsher
exclusionary punishment than white and wealthy students" (p.
123). To know this, and to take it into account, isn't opposed to a
tight focus on the situation at hand; it helps you see the situation
more clearly. In this case, the situation is a wider situation of racism and ways we discipline students of color.

Why is it important to consider this wider situation? Let's
return to Daniel Kahneman's (2011) account of human cogni-
tion. The way we describe trade-offs has a powerful impact on our
choices; when we set alternatives against each other, we make very
different choices based on how those alternatives look at a given
moment. If you ask teachers whether they want more solo planning time or smaller class sizes, they'll give a different response
than if you ask whether they want more team meeting time or
smaller class sizes, and if they want a more effective curriculum or
smaller class sizes. Humans just aren't good at translating different descriptions into the same arithmetic; the way we describe, or
frame, the trade-offs matters a huge amount. "Our preferences are
about framed problems," Kahneman writes, and "broader frames
and inclusive accounts generally lead to more rational decisions"
(p. 370). Frames have power. Framing disciplinary decisions to

include your own subconscious bias, and the harsher societal treatment of students of color, isn't part of policy, but you will interpret policy more rationally if you include them in the frame. As a school leader, you can't just wish the fear, or the racism, away.

If you came to this section for answers to student discipline, you are likely disappointed. Discipline is an area of contradictions and contains no easy, or possibly even good, answers—at least when the going gets tough. It's an area, in other words, full of trade-offs. Discipline is the hardest part of school leadership because these trade-offs are so consequential for the students involved.

I started as a principal with the intention, and the stated goal, to never expel a student. The outside view would have been—at a large middle and high school—that I wouldn't meet that goal. The outside view was right: the trade-offs meant that some students couldn't stay. Every expulsion hurt, but the trade-off was necessary.

Getting an Outside View on Data

Trade-offs can come not just from conflicting values but from a limitation we all face: the limited time we have in a day, in a school year, in the life of our school. We can't do it all. This seems so obvious that it's hardly worth saying. Yet if we don't keep that obvious fact in mind, we miss the trade-offs time forces even when the value of something seems clear. It turns out that, in a school of limited time, you can have too much of a good thing!

Data can help with trade-offs. But we're at a point, in American public education, where a key trade-off is about the data process itself. For too long, our education system failed too many kids, including far too many poor kids and kids of color, without enough public notice or accountability. To combat this, leaders of all political persuasions championed the use of testing to measure progress and drive better results. Measurement has become so common that in school districts from coast to coast you can now find calendars marked as "data days," when teachers are expected to spend time not on teaching, but on analyzing data like mid-year exams, interim assessments, teacher-created and computer-adaptive tests, as well as surveys, attendance, and behavior notes. You may or may not have a data day on your calendar, but if you work in any sort of public school, you know the pressure and time commitment of data and testing. My school effectively shut down other activities—and classes—for six days in the spring for state testing. (Not counting make-up days for kids who were absent.) The 9th graders, who didn't have testing, had six straight days of field trips so they would be out of the building and not disrupt the tests. Earlier in the year, we had six other days of testing to judge where students began in reading and math and how they were progressing according to nationwide norms. We spent a full day of teacher professional development on how to give the tests and prevent cheating. An assistant principal, along with an assessment manager, devoted the equivalent of almost two months to attending required trainings, creating testing plans, and completing forms and spreadsheets related to the state testing. And as schools go, we were one that put little emphasis on testing. Many schools (maybe yours?) also cut classes short for test-focused pep rallies!

We've slid from a reasonable, necessary, straightforward question—are the students learning?—to the current state of education leadership: school leaders and policymakers expect too much of data, overtest student learning to the detriment of learning itself, and get lost in the abundance of numbers. Decision researchers know this as the **garden path problem**: we start in a sensible direction and don't notice how that sensible path is taking us to the wrong destination. We believe in data-informed decision making—we want to know where students are and what to teach them, so we do beginning-of-year testing. We also want to know what they've learned, so we do end-of-year-testing. But the end of the year is too late to know whether what we're doing is working, so we need midyear testing. But we can't get enough information quickly enough from just one midyear test, so we do regular testing. But teachers can't spend all their time grading, so the tests need to be online and machine-gradable—that is, multiple choice. Maybe every six weeks, or every two? And if it makes sense for math, it certainly makes sense for reading. And why not science? Or music? If we're not careful, we're spending so much time testing that we don't have time to teach students what they need to learn! We've gone down the garden path with good intentions and a good first step, but we've easily moved on to the wrong place. If data is good, more data must be better. If we get into a data-driven mindset, we apply that everywhere.

The key question for leadership decision making is not "Will the data be useful?" Framing the question that way makes the answer easy and obvious: yes, you can always use more data. (An even easier question is "Will the data be interesting?" Of course it will.) Frames have power, and the proper question for leaders to ask is "Will the data help us make better enough decisions that it's worth the cost of getting and using it?" It's a question of marginal utility. Data gathering and data analysis aren't ends in themselves; they're steps—possible but not necessary steps—toward action. The downsides are in the trade-offs of each step. What else could we be doing with this data time and effort that could lead to the actual outcomes we want?

The truth is, more data won't necessarily bring better decisions. Some studies show that people overestimate how much data they'll take in before making a decision. They waste time gathering data past the point when they'll actually consider it. One of the counselors at my school wanted us to purchase a social-emotional assessment, from a leading research institution, to give to all of our students. My response when she e-mailed me: "It looks cool, yet my guess is that the cost/benefit of this won't be worthwhile. That is, the $4,000 cost, plus time to administer and use the data, and balance with other priorities, won't make enough of a difference." We knew many students who needed help. We knew that all of us adults could do a better job at providing a supportive learning environment. Would the data tell us things we didn't know? Sure. But I could use the mental simulation strategy—the various things we could find out from an additional assessment and the various ways we could respond—and realize that not much would change. The outside view told me we were already using what other schools and studies had found to be social-emotional best practices (other universal screeners, small advisory groups with a research-based curriculum, a reasonable student–counselor ratio). I said no to this new assessment; if we put the time and effort directly toward helping students, and teaching adults how to better support them, it would be a better investment.

As principal, I used data all the time, including quantitative data: student performance results, teacher and student surveys, attendance, discipline, and more. I asked, all the time, "What am I missing?" and used stack audits, surveys, and focus groups to find out. But I tried to keep in mind that gathering and analyzing more data created a time trade-off with the actual work of school improvement. And I was particularly suspicious of that trade-off when the data process focused on student assessment and involved teacher and student time. That seems paradoxical; what's more important than knowing whether students are learning? But teacher and student time come with the greatest, and clearest, trade-offs. If the students are testing, they aren't learning. If the teachers are analyzing data, they aren't teaching or planning. And the outside view—that is, research-based best practices—can already point you toward the path of instructional improvement.

Before testing more, or asking teachers to analyze more data, ask, "What am I missing?"—that is, "What more do I need so that I know how to improve student learning?" You probably already have more data than you need to make good instructional decisions. Your challenge is to make sense of what's going on, to know the best instructional practices and where they aren't happening in your school, and to push those best practices as efficiently and as hard as you can. That's not a particularly quantitative answer, but it is the most effective way to make the numbers improve.

Accepting Trade-Offs with Hiring and Evaluation

Every day of hiring season, I talked about value over replacement. I meant it to suggest a specific way of framing which people to hire, which to fire, and how to tell the difference. School leaders have choice—a limited choice—about who to put in front of our kids. One frame for that choice is blunt, even crude: "Is this teacher good or bad?" (Or, to use the faddish language of teacher evaluation systems, highly effective or minimally effective.) When we talk about **value over replacement**, the frame we use is necessarily more complex: "Is this teacher more valuable than the person I could replace her with?" In other words, hiring and firing are a form of trade-off; we balance what we have against what we think we could get.

This is a cold way to think about teachers and other staff members. It doesn't see them as ends in themselves; it acknowledges that replacements are thinkable and, indeed, should be thought about. It implies ranking: value over replacement means something is *more valuable*. To see teachers as differentiating and additive, rather than as interchangeable widgets, is not a bad thing. We feel awkward, untoward, when we place value on human beings. But the point isn't to comfort ourselves or to categorically celebrate teachers. School is for the students.

There are times to make decisions with an adult at the empathic center. When a 7th grade teacher was struggling in her marriage or when an instructional coach's brother died suddenly, I tried to respond to these situations from the most human, humane place possible. But unlike these situations, hiring and evaluation are times for cold calculation. For instance, English teachers have to pass a higher bar than math teachers; quality English teachers are easier to find. An English teacher well-liked by many students but who featured little actual reading and writing in his classes? Try as I might, I couldn't make the case to keep him. A prospective math teacher with limited training but a lot of drive? I'd rather he had experience, but I couldn't frame the decision based on a non-existent ideal; value over replacement had to win. (On the other hand, I couldn't let myself be overoptimistic about his potential. A premortem—what would it look like if he crashed and burned once in the classroom?—helped me plan for the support he needed to avoid that disaster.)

Your hiring and firing decisions are trade-offs between the value different adults bring to your students. The ways you make those decisions, and the ways you evaluate, represent a different form of trade-off: the crucial resource of time. In hiring, every moment you spend interviewing is a moment you're not attending to some other aspect of leading your school. While nothing matters more than getting the right teachers on your team, you have to consider the costs of additional procedural steps as well as benefits. Sample lessons in front of your own students, for instance, are wonderful, but they take a ton of time to set up and observe. Are they worth it? Maybe, but you can't just say, "They're wonderful," and leave it at that. Limited time makes trade-offs.

The same trade-offs occur, when evaluation time comes around, for teachers you already have. Before I was an assistant principal in the Washington, D.C., Public Schools, I worked in the

DCPS central office, helping with Michelle Rhee's signature new teacher evaluation system, IMPACT. We used multiple rigorous observations and value-added calculations to give every teacher numerical scores, which combined into a master numerical score for every teacher across the school district—recommending whether they kept their job, they got a bonus, or they were fired. The first year, we fired more than 200 teachers with IMPACT. We were going to change the education world through evaluation.

When I became founding principal of a charter school, though, I did the opposite of IMPACT because I saw the trade-offs it implied. In almost every case, the purpose of a formal evaluation is to tell employees their formal status. It's the center of a key decision: to retain the teacher or not. I didn't need a complex numerical system to decide that. (These weren't easy decisions, as noted above, but complex math or an in-depth formal rubric wasn't going to help!) We also didn't need a rubric to talk about instruction. In fact, tying a rubric to numerical evaluation, and evaluation to job security, meant the IMPACT conversations weren't about instruction—they were about the numbers and the rubric. Replacing a more complex evaluation with a simple one made room for more valuable instructional conversation and feedback.

The more intense the rubric and evaluation process, the greater the focus on that process. Teachers end up focused on their own numbers, and that's not the same as focused on teaching and learning. Even if you have a district-mandated formal evaluation process (not everyone is in a start-up charter school), watch out for its unintended effects. Its main power is to fire people who shouldn't be teaching. But it also has the power to undermine improvement conversations for those people who should.

The other problem with an intense evaluation process is the time it takes. If it's the teachers' time—if, for instance, they have to produce an elaborate portfolio of artifacts exemplifying each element of their job—consider what else they could be doing with their time: planning, grading, tutoring, sleeping. Yes, the process makes them more reflective, absolutely! But what's the trade-off? If you're anything like me, you've spent inordinate amounts of time writing more extensive evaluation reports than you can count, and you're pretty sure most of them, even if they got a reaction from the teacher, didn't lead to improved action in the classroom. And sleeping might sound pretty good.

Getting an Outside View About Your Teachers' Time

Bored office workers sometimes make up work to seem busy. But nobody at a school has to make up work to do; the things that feel absolutely crucial are never ending. Any time we ask teachers—or schools—to do something new, we need to ask, at what cost?

You may want teachers to meet across teams, provide a new report to parents, or implement a new program. These may all be good things to do. But unless you imagine that teachers have extra time in their days (with or without students), all come with a downside: they will take away from things teachers are already doing. That may be other meetings, other phone calls to parents, or other programs; that may be exercise, family time, or Netflix. Or sleep! *Something* will get squeezed. Sometimes it's quality: the new program and the old one are both implemented, but neither well. Sometimes it's work–life balance; as I know from my own experience, there are charter schools that get young teachers to work 12-plus hours a day (but never for many years). Usually, the trade-off is with whatever the individual teacher decides is the lowest priority. I spoke to one elementary principal who knew her teachers were supposed to be e-mailing parents weekly but weren't; she knew they were supposed to be checking students' book baggies but weren't; she knew they were supposed to be making students keep reading logs but weren't. The principal knew she was asking too much of teachers and knew they weren't keeping up. She knew there were trade-offs. She just refused to make the trade-offs herself.

If there is something you want teachers, or other staff, to do, and if you are willing to recognize the reality of trade-offs, you have three possible directives for those teachers. The most straightforward is the message of the charter school where I taught early in my career: work harder. The work is extra important; your students are worth it; you need to do more (more than the kids usually get, more than you used to do, more than other teachers might do). If you have a sufficiently inspirational message and a sufficiently committed, energetic, and child-free staff, this can work. You can avoid time trade-offs, at least for a while! But your committed, energetic, and child-free staff will burn out, grow up, and have children of their own, and you'll have to hire new staff to take their place, with all the trade-offs turnover implies. You can also choose a shorter-run message to work harder: put in more hours for this month, for the rest of this year, until the state tests. This only works in the short term, of course, and not so many times, before burnout becomes systemic (and your teachers stop believing you about the short-run part).

The second possible choice is to say work smarter, not harder. It's an easier message, but it's also hard to actually do, and saying it can make teachers roll their eyes hard enough to knock an unwary principal over! Work smarter, not harder so rarely comes with guidance on what that actually means; the saying denigrates the intelligence of the audience (are they are too dumb to have thought to themselves, maybe, "I should work smarter"?) while giving nothing new. If you mean for your staff to work smarter, not harder, you need to give them tools, not slogans, that can make what they're already doing more efficient. Shifting tasks to technology or to students—grading software that automatically updates parents about missing assignments, or ways to get students to do the busy work of managing a classroom—can actually help teachers save time. But usually, what we mean when we say work smarter, not harder is that we want teachers to do more in the same amount of time, but we don't know how.

A better choice is to accept trade-offs and give your teachers permission to make trade-offs too. This message is best phrased as **do this, not that**. You know that not everything is possible. Your teachers know it too, so everyone can stop pretending. You have priorities; these priorities have to take precedence; some things just won't get done. It's OK; everything never gets done! Especially when introducing a new requirement, eliminate an old one. You'll bring clarity and, in place of eye-rolling, a sigh of relief.

How do you know what not to do? Ask teachers what they think is pointless; even better, ask them what they know they're supposed to do but never bother and just feel guilty about. One easy place to eliminate time: paperwork and documentation. Too often, schools build reporting systems on top of reporting systems and don't think through process improvements that can save teachers from double- and triple-entering the same information in redundant systems. When I was assistant principal, our teachers, who entered attendance on their computers every day, at the end of the year also had to complete an index card, clearly left over from the 1970s, showing annual attendance for each of their students. (It was only their year-end exhaustion that saved us from revolution.) Many things you stop doing will be more painful. Clubs and athletics are important, but to have teachers leading them brings a trade-off with academics. Playground duty in elementary schools and dance attendance in high schools force their own trade-offs. Like some forms of documentation, these nonclassroom responsibilities may be necessary. That doesn't mean they're cost-free.

Even with paperwork, there will be some who see the purpose in the old requirement, who have faithfully kept to it, and who will protest, or at least mourn, its loss. This is OK, and natural; it was there for a reason. Nobody at a school is digging holes just to fill them in! Fear of confronting loss and admitting that not every-thing can be done keep schools from recognizing trade-offs. The necessary element is bravery, the willingness to say that we have to choose. That's also known as leadership.

Getting an Outside View About Your Own Time

And even if you make reasonable choices for your teachers, the worst trade-offs to confront are how you allocate your own time and energy. There's no accountant's budget here, but the bottom line still exists: there is only so much of you to go around. And sadly, I have no magic potion or genie's lamp. There cannot be more of you. There cannot be more time in the day. There are systems, there are workshops, there are books about time management, you can learn tricks, and you can do better. But there will only be one you, and there will only be 24 hours in a day. (And you'd better be sleeping and having a nonwork life during a substantial portion of those 24!) All the improved time management you can muster will not change the need for trade-offs in how you use your time.

Two frames can help you see these trade-offs more clearly: the outside view and satisficing. How can the outside view help with time trade-offs? When we think about what makes a great school, we can see whether the way we *do* spend our time aligns to the way we *should* spend our time—if, that is, what we're trying to do is make a great school! In his book *Leading with Focus* (2016), Mike Schmoker calls for simplicity in leadership: "a tight, near-exclusive focus on the lowest possible number of the most effec-tive and manageable actions and expectations" (p. 5). Schmoker's model of leadership is for you to ensure three levers: "a coherent, content-rich curriculum; a solid amount of traditional literacy tasks and activities; [and] effective, soundly structured lessons" (p. 6). (I would add positive student culture as a fourth essential element.) He notes that "the power of these three elements has overwhelmingly been established by research—as has the evidence that they are manifestly rare in schools" (p. 6). Why are they rare? I believe it is because leaders don't focus on them. Instead, there are buses to coordinate, field trips to approve, adult squabbles to mediate, parents to assuage . . . you can make your own list; I'm sure it's long! This list distracts great leaders, leading great schools, from their focus.

Does the way you spend your days improve those essential elements? What would an outside view predict? Even if you have different essential elements, different priorities, would an outside view predict that your time will move them forward? Most likely, the essential elements are important but not urgent, and it's the rare school leader who gets to them on a daily basis. The trade-offs you make every day—if you are like most school leaders—instead prioritize the minor crises, all the urgencies in the life of a school, while you let the big things slide. An outside view would predict that such a trade-off leads to a well-managed school but not a great one. A coordinated bus system is common across American schools. Effective, soundly structured lessons are not.

Your leadership alone can't change that. Somebody has to coordinate the buses! That's where **satisficing** comes in. It's a funny word, but it's one of the most crucial for saving your sanity as an effective leader. To satisfice is to find an acceptable path—not the best, just acceptable—and to move forward. To satisfice is to lower your standards. And I want to urge you to lower your standards . . . on the little things. If the buses are a few minutes late, if the field trip is a little scattered, as long as no kid gets lost, it's OK. Can you accept OK? Can you accept those imperfections, if the outside view of trade-offs suggests that making them better would reduce your chance of improving the big things?

Satisficing is hard for school leaders because, almost by definition, school leaders are highly effective people. You didn't get to where you are by letting the little things slide. You have high standards for yourself. But when you are responsible for a school building as a whole, for the entire complex and wild system, not everything will be right. You will have to delegate to people who may do a worse job than you would. You will see imperfection almost everywhere you look. And the temptation will be to make as many things right as you can, to find as many places where you can raise what's happening to your own high standards. But those will be the little things, and they will keep you from pushing forward on the big things. Getting the little things absolutely right provides a moment's pleasure, but in the long run, that won't get you past mediocre. There are trade-offs.

So where do you put your highly effective energy, and where do you satisfice? The answer depends on your context, of course. But even more than context, your values should determine this trade-off: what matters most to you and where you matter most. What matters most to you? Maybe it's literacy, student engagement, and equity. Maybe it's critical thinking, emotional well-being, and community service. Notice that these are short lists; only so many big rocks can fit in your bucket before it overflows. For these big rocks, aim not to satisfice; aim for the best these highest-value priorities can be. And notice who's carrying those big rocks: where do you matter most? If literacy is a top priority but you have an excellent instructional coach solely focused on that priority, you may not add enough value to place your time there. If community service is crucial but your school's program is running smoothly, then it may matter to you, but your energy doesn't matter enough for it. Sure, if you got into the details, you could likely make it better, but it would be at too great a cost. Beware the trade-off. Satisfice more.

This is, to put it mildly, so hard. So, so hard. As one principal emailed me recently, "I just want to make sure I'm always well-planned, and I'm still feeling like I'm behind." The truth is, as principal, she will *never* not feel like she's behind. She will always actually be behind! Trade-offs are inevitable. The only things that will help are to accept that fact, let go of feeling bad about it, and see the big picture and have confidence that you're improving it. I know that kids' lives are at stake. But everything can't always be an emergency. You can only survive by balancing optimism, realism, and hope.

DON'T FORGET

In a school, there's no such thing as perfection. Trade-offs are inevitable. The challenge is to consciously make the trade-offs you want.

- It's possible things will go wrong. Use a premortem to imagine the path toward failure so you can avoid missteps.
- Use a mental simulation strategy to play out how others will react to your decisions and how those reactions will lead to other reactions. Remember the limits of your control.
- The outside view can be more realistic; compare your situation to other, similar situations to understand likely outcomes.
- Frames have power. When considering trade-offs, your decision will be shaped by what factors you include in the trade-off, so use as broad a frame as possible.
- The hardest trade-offs are with time and energy. For teachers, remember they likely feel at their limit; move them forward with the directive to do this, not that. For yourself, satisficing can help; your standard for most smaller matters should be what's acceptable rather than the best they can be.

- Identify what matters most to you and where you matter most; those are the areas to put your energy. Satisfice everywhere else. But satisficing is no magic bullet; there is no magic gift of more time, which is why trade-offs are so common and so crucial to confront.

KNOW YOURSELF

You wouldn't work in a school if you didn't believe in better possibilities. But our optimism can prevent us from seeing trade-offs. Consider how realistic your vision is.

- Are you usually more optimistic than the people around you? Or less? How do you use others to help you balance your own tendencies?
- What strategies do you use to see down the road and anticipate consequences of your decisions?
- Do you think that your school is more successful at making changes than most other schools? Why? What if you're wrong?
- Where have you noticed trade-offs in discipline, data usage, or hiring and evaluation? What hidden trade-offs might you not have seen?
- What trade-offs are your teachers making and hoping nobody notices? What trade-offs would you rather they make? How can you make those trade-offs explicit and redirect their time?
- Would your colleagues describe you as a perfectionist? Would they be right? In the last week, what did you spend time improving that would have been acceptable at lower quality?
- What matters most to you at your school, and where does your involvement make the most difference? In what lower-priority areas can satisficing help save your time and energy for what's most important?

Question 4

Does It Have to Be This Way?

So far in this book, I might seem like a downer. You're missing things. You can only take small steps. You need to watch out for pitfalls and false positives. You have to accept trade-offs and downsides.

But thinking realistically about trade-offs can be overdone when our thinking is limited by our experience. We slip into cynicism when all we are able to see is all there *is*, instead of all that *could be*. At an early age, the structures of school imprinted on us certain assumptions: This is what a classroom is. This is what a teacher is. This is what a student, what homework, what a test, what a school day, what learning is. We know so well—too well—how things go. And we falter when we cannot think outside of what we've known.

To ask, "Does it have to be this way?" is to open up your vision. It is both an announcement of and a push toward freedom, removing blinders and loosening mental chains. The school is an artificial structure, our society's current best guess at how to grow human beings from early childhood to adulthood in a reasonably economical and systematic way. We confuse that artifice with nature's laws, and "Does it have to be this way?" rejects such confusion.

In practical terms, to ask this question is to open up decisions for your school driven not by how schools operated in the past, but by what's best for kids *now*.

When I was a child in elementary school, we learned about timelines through a classic activity. The teacher herded the class into the hallway carrying a giant roll of masking tape. We started at one end with the Big Bang. The masking tape went down, down, down the hallway. About halfway, we marked the origins of the earth. Down the hallway, we unrolled to the first single-celled organism, down to the age of dinosaurs, much further down to hominids, to *Homo sapiens*, and down to agriculture and so on. Our whole country, the United States, was squinched up at the very edge of the wall. We stood against the wall and peered down the length of the school, our whole little world, and sensed—as the teacher intended—the enormity of history and just how tiny all we knew seemed in the scope of the whole.

If we'd added the peak of the one-room schoolhouse, it would have been even closer to the wall than the squinch of the United States. The rise of the public school as we know it, with multiple separate grades and everyone expected to go, would be halfway between the start of the squinch and now. The fat yellow pencils we used wouldn't have been able to mark such a narrow band.

To the broad question, "Does it have to be this way?" the answer, in historical perspective, is surely no. In our own little squinch of history, though, as much as we want to be free, it's a lot harder to make a different mark.

THE WRONG PATH: THE CROWD SEEMS SAFE

Fashions change over time. Once, elite college students attended class in a sport jacket and tie (they were all men, of

CONTINUED

course). Now T-shirts and jeans are the rule, and if you show up at a 9:00 a.m. lecture in jacket and tie, there'd better be a joke or a job interview involved. In middle schools, on the other hand, jeans are less and less common; athletic pants and leggings have taken over. When I was in middle school, there was a brief craze for "hypercolor" T-shirts, which changed color (mine went from blue to pink) when someone pressed their hand against the fabric. It was a terrific technology for flirting that lasted about three loads of laundry and for a few months in 1991. Hypercolor hasn't been seen since.

Middle school fashion can confuse adults. (That's often the intention.) But if you're a middle school student concerned with fitting in, fashion isn't that hard; just look around at what everyone else has on. It might be different from a generation ago; it might be different a generation from now; it might be comfortable or uncomfortable, revealing or covering; but if your clothes accord with the norm, then your clothes, at least, won't be questioned. Nobody will ask why you're wearing a hypercolor shirt if everyone else is wearing a hypercolor shirt too.

You, as an adult and school leader, are thinking independently about consequential things like curriculum and scheduling and assessments, not hypercolor shirts! But the tug of conformity exists for you too. It's called **social legitimacy**, the substitution of normalcy for other standards of judgment. If your curriculum and schedule and assessments are pretty much like everyone else's, that seems good enough.

The tug of conformity is hard to overcome. The pains of middle school are still with us; most of us want to fit in, not to answer questions about why our outfit looks so different or to explain our larger counter-trend choices. Nobody will ask why your schedule is the way it is if it's the same as all the other schools'.

The difference from fashion is that a jacket and tie, jeans, and leggings will all pretty much keep you warm. But unless fitting in is your aim, a different schedule might actually do the job better! That's hard to keep in mind. As one sociology-of-education textbook (Brint, 2017) says, "A school may or may not educate students effectively, but if it faithfully mirrors the organization of other schools, it will be accorded legitimacy in the eyes of the public" (p. 15). We've seen some teenage fashions that, in retrospect, look ridiculous: try an 80s music video for a laugh. But at the time, who would point it out when everybody was doing it?

Social legitimacy means that nobody will tell you you're doing something wrong if they're doing the same. But that's different from doing it right—if what you care about is what's good for children rather than what everyone else is doing. Sooner or later, that hypercolor is bound to fade.

How to Change Perspective

How can we see outside the limits we've known? How can we exchange our hypercolor T-shirts for a new outfit, not one that matches current fashion trends but one that best meets the needs we see? So much of principals' thinking is restricted to the daily grind of getting our schools through to the last bell. I want to challenge you to think differently. Later in this chapter, I'll give three examples of educational practices that will look different in the future. First, I'll explain three methods you can use to change your perspective: getting down to core values, using integrative thinking, and applying an anthropological lens.

We can see past today's structures if we look for the reasons they exist—not the ways we do things but the *why* behind them. When we **get down to core values**, we can rebuild from a stronger foundation. For instance, is recess a problematic point in your school day? Well, does recess actually need to exist? Or are there other ways to get at, and recombine, the core values of outdoor time and physical activity? Another way to conceptualize this form of questioning is to think from first principles—not principal as in school leader, but rather, the kind of *values* you work from. Recess isn't a first principle; we don't value recess itself (or do we think children need recess on a Saturday?). Physical activity and outdoor time, on the other hand, are first principles: as the parent of a high-energy elementary schooler, I can say any day missing these is a very difficult day for both of us!

Getting down to core values can be an answer to trade-offs, which are sometimes about surface structures rather than the core values beneath them. In *Creating Great Choices* (2017), Jennifer Riel and Roger Martin describe what they call **integrative thinking**: identify the principles underlying each side of a trade-off and look for ways to integrate those principles to eliminate the trade-off. If lead teachers find planning time during recess, but lack of supervision means playground games get rowdy and some kids are excluded, that looks like a trade-off. If you make the lead teachers supervise recess, those teachers will resist (and you might violate a union contract); if you eliminate recess, parents and kids will revolt. But the parents and kids aren't revolting because they like recess as a structure; it's because kids like running around outside! Some schools have implemented structured games led by classroom aides or parent volunteers; it's not quite recess, but these structures can actually respond better to the core value of physical activity if more students start to play. They don't, though, fulfill the core value of child-directed play—if that is, indeed, core. What are the core values of your school's recess?

We can see integrative thinking—or, at least, attempts at it—in many pedagogical innovations. For teenagers at risk of dropping out, career exploration can provide a reason to stay in school, but many of these students lack core academic skills. There's an obvious trade-off between internships or job shadowing and classroom time for building skills. I work with one high school that is shifting to a career and technical education (CTE) model and redesigning English and math classes from the ground up, with curriculum built around a culinary pathway, an early-childhood-education pathway, and a construction-trades pathway. (The construction-trades pathway, using integrative thinking, includes a geometry-intensive math approach and reading building codes and safety regulations as classroom texts.) The core values at this school are for students to build literacy and numerical skills and connect their current tasks to a better future. Neither the traditional curriculum nor internships are core values. Integrative thinking provides, in this case, a model for curricular integration as well.

There are, of course, plenty of ways this approach could fall short. Plenty of curricular innovations do! Integrative thinking isn't actually integrative when it masks, rather than resolves, the underlying trade-offs. Another school wanted to move toward more student-centered, project-based instruction. Frustrated by the lack of progress, the leadership planned a two-week innovation project where kids designed solutions to the trash littering their city—solutions, that is, prototyped with toilet paper rolls, pipe cleaners, and yarn. This was student-centered, all right, and highly engaging and fun. After the two weeks, the students had prototypes, but it wasn't clear what they'd actually learned. This happens at innovative schools around the country: creativity without clarity that more than one core value is usually at stake, leading to projects disconnected from content. Sometimes, with careful planning and rigorous reflection, trade-offs can be avoided. But innovation alone won't do it.

This is why identifying those core values is so important. Most school structures are accretions of values and habits from what was once easiest, what once made sense. They were other people's answers to the trade-offs of their time. As long as you see the trade-offs at stake, you have the ability to devise your own new answers.

You can also learn new things from different people's answers to trade-offs if you look to, and think about, *really* different people. Remember that masking-tape timeline? The earliest *Homo sapiens* skeletons are almost 200,000 years old. For all that time, humans have been raising their young—that is, teaching them. The first city we know of, Uruk in Mesopotamia, was founded in approximately 4500 BCE. For all of that time, there have been enough children in a single place at a single time that it made sense to bring them together to learn. What we know now as *school* is but one way of doing this elemental human activity. The **anthropological lens** can show us other possibilities.

It's become common to look to schools in other countries for ideas about improving our own. The Program for International Student Assessment (PISA) shows which do better on standardized tests; we're impressed by Japanese lesson planning and Finland's esteem for teachers. But the anthropological lens lets us see not just how other countries do school but also how other societies have approached the entire educational enterprise. School—a building where children go, isolated from other activities of a society, to be taught a curriculum by adults whose profession is teaching—is not, after all, anywhere near universal. In fact, such a practice is historically unusual. Far more common is what one 20th-century Hopi Indian recalled about his childhood before his people's society was colonized: "Learning to work was like play. We children tagged around with our elders and copied what they did" (Gaskins & Paradise, 2010, p. 89). Much learning outside of schools is still like that—observation and imitation of an activity without a core purpose of learning. It's how we learn to cook, to clean a house, to navigate our hometown. My point is not that apprenticeship should be the new model for school (though that's not a bad idea)—it's that some aspects of human learning are common enough to be seen as natural, but the way schools work is not.

With an anthropological lens, you can ask how else societies have done what your school is trying to do. Another way to put it is what you think about human nature—what is common across societies—and how your school can do more of that. Skills in areas such as poetic devices, civic participation, technology usage, local history, and artistic production occur throughout human societies. Without a school, how do these happen? We can look at out-of-school learning in our own society for inspiration as well. How do children learn to play instruments, ride bikes, or take care of younger siblings? How do they gain competence at Pokémon, fan fiction, or double Dutch? What new possibilities do these examples show you?

You may not have any idea how hunter-gatherers raised their children. The act of imagining (as long as you don't mistake that imagination for anthropological truth) can itself be helpful when you cast yourself outside of your specific situation. So imagine how a hunter-gatherer might critique your school, and consider what would make sense versus what might just seem nuts. In the cafeteria, for instance, scores, sometimes hundreds, of young human beings of a similar age group are eating at large indoor tables at a designated time of day, five days a week—what a bizarre idea! How incomprehensible it would have been even two hundred years ago in the United States! How strange it would still be in much of the world! You could explain or defend some of the "nuts" parts of your school, but what would, with the anthropological lens, not actually make sense to you? (Does anybody, adult or child, enjoy the noise and intensity of the cafeteria? Maybe there is some other way, given the resources available, you could organize lunch.) What might you change if you could see it anew?

Questions That Challenge the Status Quo

While it can be intimidating to re-envision entire areas of education at your school, it can also be incredibly rewarding—and more possible than you think! Using integrative thinking, applying an anthropological lens, and keeping core values at the center will help you make decisions that carve out new directions to move your school forward. These strategies have helped me make better decisions about the areas of my work that challenged me most: grading, special education, and technology use.

Deciding the Future of Grading with Integrative Thinking

The masking tape we used in elementary school to mark the history of the universe was intended to illustrate the unimaginable vastness of time. A 4th grader could look at that scale—the hallway he traversed daily—and see 8 billion years. We weren't meant to confuse the model for the real thing, but the marks on the tape did embed in us a particular way to conceptualize the world according to school. In British schools, *marks* refer to what we call *grades*, the numbers or letters or percentages meant to tell students (and, of course, their parents) where they are. Writing teachers mark up papers. Students are marked down for their flaws. We mark, or grade, to make learning legible; grading is a complex and evolving process put down on paper, reduced and simplified to easy-to-comprehend notations in which so much is often lost.

There's nothing that seems more obvious—more socially legitimate—than grading students. Red pens, report cards, and transcripts are both the machinery and the output of schools, the ways we do business and the signs that business has been done. They are also a prime example of the need to get down to core values. Why do we grade, and why do we grade as we do? In *On Your Mark: Challenging the Conventions of Grading and Reporting*, Thomas Guskey (2015) notes that we have two fundamental reasons for grading: "to discriminate among students and to identify differences in their performance," and to "reflect the degree to which students have learned, accomplished, or achieved what they were taught." The first is the **normative** purpose; the second is the **criterion** purpose. If students get a range of grades—some at the top of the class, some at the bottom, some in the middle—the normative purpose is fulfilled. If everyone learns, and everyone scores well, the normative purpose is missed, but the criterion purpose can be fulfilled. Is a system of grades in which everyone gets an *A* necessarily a failure? From the normative perspective, yes. How will we know who's at the top of the class? But is knowing who's on top our core value?

As most teachers and schools do it, grades represent a mixture of norms and criteria. Teachers would be happy if everyone earned an *A*, they say, but the classrooms in which everyone does are few and far between (and the students and teachers down the hall will all agree that it's because the class is an easy *A*, not because every student has learned, accomplished, or achieved what they should!). Mixture and confusion are, in fact, the hallmarks of most American grading. Our grades reflect both how the student is doing in *learning each subject area*, and how the student is doing in *learning to be a student*. Traditional grades mix these things and end up unclear about both: Is a student getting a *B+* because he did all the homework, because the teacher likes her, because she's a good test taker, because he participates in class, because she knows 88 percent of the material? We have a system—relatively new because grades as we have them were basically unknown before the 20th century—in which we stuff everything we care about into a blender and pour out a single mark on a report card. That's what happens when core values get confused. You can, after all, learn math without doing any homework or do all your homework and still not learn math, although most math teachers would say both learning math and doing homework are important!

Social legitimacy can mask underlying disagreements on core values. If you give students grades, everyone agrees that's what you should do. If you give *this* student *this* grade, though, the student or the parent might think it's too low; the teacher down the hall, who taught the student last year, might think it's too high. Disagreement in particular instances can suggest when the social legitimacy of a practice might hide more fundamental conflict in the principles. Remember "What am I missing?" and listen to the dissenters.

When multiple core values are at stake, integrative thinking suggests that clarity on them can lead to new structures that eliminate trade-offs. The conflict comes from the limitations of the way we do things, not the values themselves. Which is more important for a student: getting the right result, working hard, or improving? Each of these is separate, important, and deserving of feedback. One grading scale, whether A through F or 0 through 100, collapses their distinctions, forcing painful (though, in our current system, often invisible) trade-offs. Thomas Guskey suggests, instead, separate criteria and grades for product (what students know and are able to do at a particular point in time), process (student habits like participation and completed homework), and individualized progress (how much students have gained or how much they have improved over a particular period of time). That sounds like more grading work for teachers, though, of course, many factors contribute to the one grade most students now get. But it also sounds a lot clearer to parents and students, who understand the values behind the marks. It's also a way to Fermi-ize the problem of grading: break it down into component parts and improve each part!

At the middle school where I was principal, we used the International Baccalaureate grading scale with our own additions. In each subject, students got grades on standards-based criteria, with scores on a 1 through 8 scale. As I explained to parents (and re-explained every marking period!), a 5 was a good grade, and an 8, while possible, was very rare and not the expectation; the scale went higher than "good," in part, to show that even top achievers had room to grow. These subject-area grades showed the current level of achievement, not an average and without habits like participation or homework completion. For those, we also had separate "approaches to learning" grades to which multiple teachers contributed so that students received feedback on areas like collaboration and self-management. Both subject-area mastery and approaches to learning were core values of the school, and we celebrated achievement in each area with honor rolls and end-of-year awards. As you can imagine, the same students didn't always do well in both! We achieved integrative thinking, in this case, by separating out our core values rather than forcing them into a single muddle.

Keeping Core Values at the Center with Special Education

The systems through which we educate students with disabilities—like the phrase "students with disabilities" itself—is a much more recent creation than the report card. It wasn't until 1975 that the Education for All Handicapped Children Act introduced a federal right of ("handicapped") children to receive a free, appropriate public education. The history of education of students with disabilities before then, at least in American public schools, is largely a history of exclusion: separate classrooms, separate floors in school buildings, separate school buildings, or no education at all. The Education for All Handicapped Children Act, and its later incarnation as the Individuals with Disabilities Education Act (IDEA), required both individualized education programs and that these kids be educated, to the greatest extent possible, with their peers.

These changes were the result of advocates asking, "Does it have to be this way?" and pushing for change. Just because students with cerebral palsy, deafness, or epilepsy had been excluded in the past was no reason to continue that exclusion. Along with legislators and judges, these educators and parents got down to core values—in particular, the right of all children to achieve their full potential and be part of society—and built from there.

What they built, though, is no more permanent than the previous regime. Special education has grown into a thicket of regulations and processes that school leaders either learn to navigate or face reprimands and lawsuits. (Somebody needs to guide you. If you don't have an in-house expert, find or grow one.) That thicket's growth is not natural; it's an outcome of legislative compromises, bureaucratic necessities, judicial fiats, and the actual needs and lives of children.

In the decade between 2005 and 2015, the number of students deemed to have autism in the United States more than doubled. Starting in 1994, with the fourth edition of the *Diagnostic and Statistical Manual of Mental Disorders*, some children had Asperger's syndrome; after the fifth edition in 2013, no children did, because Asperger's no longer existed (and was instead incorporated under a single diagnostic category of autism spectrum disorder) (Barahona-Corrêa & Filipe, 2016). Did nature, or the nature of children, change in that time? No, the systems we use to classify them did. Birthdays fall randomly on the calendar, and our definitions are often just as fickle. Students born in August are identified as having ADHD at a significantly higher rate than students born in September. Is it possible that students born in September are less affected than students born a few weeks before? No. In some states, the youngest children in a grade are those born just before September 1. If you're younger and less mature than your classmates, you're more likely to fit the criteria of ADHD when parents raise concerns or when teachers complete assessment forms (Jena, Barnett, & Layton, 2018).

Our special education system is artificial, including the ways we think about students. What it means to *be* a student with disabilities is to be *identified* as a student with disabilities. That's it. The category of students with disabilities, like the category of Asperger's syndrome, is a human creation. It has been recreated numerous times since 1975. It will be again. As educators navigate the thicket, they should look around and think; it doesn't have to be this way.

Special education as we know it is an artificial answer to the very real challenge of human variability. The anthropological lens can help. Every society has a range of people, with a range of physical, mental, and emotional characteristics. Before Asperger's was named, the range of characteristics we briefly called Asperger's existed. Before and after September 1, in any given year, the range of human characteristics exists. In Fiji and in France, ten thousand years in the past and a century from now, humans vary. The labels we now give that variety, like the acronyms and rules and meetings that govern special education, do not cross place and time, but human variety is universal. The most extreme cases of human variability create challenges for any society, especially for the parents who want their children to thrive, but many of the challenges we face with special education come from trying to fit normal human variability into the rigidities of our system.

The anthropological lens can provide motivation and guidance for the decisions you make on a day-to-day basis. Inclusion is still a controversy in many schools that hold on to a system of separate, self-contained classes even for students with mild or specific learning disabilities. But from the perspective of a hunter-gatherer, such separation doesn't make sense; the tribe has to figure out how to include the child, and the child has to learn how to keep up with the tribe. That doesn't mean it's easy! (Or that there's never a need for self-contained classes.) Rather, it's a way of seeing a student with a disability as part of the tribe—that is, *included*—as the default rather than letting our present system's artificial labeling dictate what we see. The anthropological lens can also help us see students' particular needs without a label. At my school, thanks to a unique teacher's skills and interest, we piloted a semester-long behavior support class to teach social and executive-functioning skills to high-needs students. The class provided IEP hours in the social-emotional category. But the class also included students without IEPs, if they'd demonstrated sufficient behavior need— in other words, if they'd caused enough trouble! The teacher was a special education teacher, but with the anthropological lens, it wasn't a special education class. Instead, it was a way of teaching some of our children how to keep up with the tribe.

That was our core value, after all: as much as we recognized the artificiality of our structure, we also believed in helping as many students as possible succeed within it. In special education's here and now, as opposed to its future, many of our leadership decisions are about placement. This is true for students, but it's also true for teachers. Who will have what class, and, often, with what co-teacher or aide? As a secondary school principal, I faced a frustration many leaders know: co-teaching English and math classes rarely seemed worth it. Getting teachers to actually share the work was part matchmaking, part marriage counseling. (And sometimes divorce mediation: "Can you pretend to be amicable for the sake of the children?") Even the best pairs often fell into a lead-and-support model, with the general education teacher at the front of the class and the special education teacher assisting during independent work time and redirecting off-task kids. It was a waste of the second teacher's expertise and also, frankly, of money. Why was I paying a teacher salary for an aide's work? Did it have to be this way?

Co-teaching was not a core value. And co-teaching was not, in fact, on any student's IEP. What the IEPs called for was specialized instruction in a general education setting. We could, I realized, get down to the core values: instruction that was skilled and individualized enough to meet student needs, backed by deep content knowledge, without isolating students with disabilities from their peers. (Co-teaching may be a core value for somebody, but it wasn't for us!) We called our answer dual certification. General education teachers received training in differentiation and took the special education Praxis; special education teachers took content-area refresher courses and the content-area Praxis. Then, rather than one class of twenty or twenty-five students and two teachers, we scheduled one class of fifteen students and one dual-certified teacher. We paid the single teacher an extra stipend (the budget still worked), and we avoided the dysfunctional marriages and silent teachers at the back of the room that co-teaching so often involves.

The point isn't for you to use our solution. There were still trade-offs; for instance, we had to add aides to some classes that, even though smaller, still required a second adult for behavior support. Rather, the point is that, if you start from core values rather than the way things are, you can come up with your own solutions. It's far better than approaching special education from the starting point of rules and regulations, which makes it a process of box-checking rather than noticing and developing the individuality of students. We must remind ourselves to see past the thicket to the actual, variable human beings that the thicket is meant to protect but too often constricts. When we find ourselves stuck in a pattern that isn't working, it's time to ask, "Does it have to be this way?"

Bringing an Anthropological Lens to Decisions on Technology

As much as the internet seems to open new possibilities and invite a decisive break from the past, the same lesson holds for thinking about technology: only by understanding history can we find another way. Throughout the last century, attempts to change the fundamentals of how classrooms work have foundered on the seemingly immovable rocks of traditional practice. Yes, there are aspects of tradition that technology can improve incrementally. But to make a big difference, technology has to be accompanied by big changes to the traditional roles for teachers and curriculum.

After a career in public education and a master's degree in technology and innovation, I led a new school founded with a 1:1 Chromebook program. We gave every student a computer, which they kept 24 hours a day, 7 days a week, 365 days a year. We had students who knew how to code and students who, on the first day, didn't know how to type a capital letter on the keyboard. (By the second year, we learned not to use the default Password123 so that students didn't have to type a capital P on the first day!)

Our students learned very quickly. Those same students who couldn't make capital letters were, soon enough, listening to the latest music on Spotify, chatting with friends on Google Hangouts, and trying (sometimes successfully) to find ways around our content filters. But our technology—even the most up to date and enabled with high-speed internet—changed very little about teaching and learning.

If I'd paid attention to education history, I wouldn't be surprised. For a century before the internet, as historians David Tyack and Larry Cuban (1995) describe, reformers attempted to "use time, space, and numbers of students as flexible resources and to diversify uniform class periods, same-sized rooms, and standard class sizes" (p. 87). In other words, reformers were trying to personalize learning—just like today's technological futurists!

Those of us who want to see dramatically different outcomes from schools are susceptible to an overly simple theory: change the inputs, change the outcome. If we update technology, we'll update student learning. But the techno-optimists who look at wired classrooms and proclaim *revolution* underestimate the counterrevolutionary power of educational conservatism. One hundred years ago, at the dawn of motion pictures, Thomas Edison proclaimed that books would soon be obsolete in the schools (Berger, 2005). Today, schools remain one of the few American institutions that operate in the same basic ways as they did in the steamship era, especially what happens in the classroom. Why is it so difficult to change schools?

Start with complexity. When business guru Clayton Christensen turned his attention to school systems, he identified four "interdependences": temporal, lateral, physical, and hierarchical (Christensen, Horn, & Johnson, 2008). School is structured to go in a certain order (grade by grade), with certain subjects related to other subjects, with classrooms of certain shapes and sizes, with specific relationships between teacher, principal, district, state, and federal law. This complex order manages huge numbers of kids at once, all complex in their own right and in their relationships with each other, and such a complex system can overwhelm any small lever for change.

Teachers also lack the time, space, and support to experiment with innovation. Every minute matters in a school, and every student matters; you don't get do-overs for 7th grade, and schools don't have research labs for teachers to try out innovations. Instead, teachers turn to what they know best: the way they were taught and the way the people around them are teaching. Schools tend to have conservative cultures. School is, almost by definition, where the experience of the past is transmitted to the future. People who choose to spend their adult lives in classrooms usually had good experience in classrooms as children; school worked for them as it was. There is also the constant feeling that adults in a school—overwhelmingly outnumbered, after all, by children—must be a united force for order. Teachers fear anarchy above all. So the students can carry around school-issued Chromebooks, but they still have to spend their time listening to the teacher or paraphrasing the textbook—or, perhaps, using the Chromebook to paraphrase the electronic textbook. Using computers in socially legitimate ways makes everyone involved breathe a little easier.

The difficulty of big change doesn't imply that small changes aren't worth making. In explaining my school's use of Chromebooks to prospective parents—usually of 5th graders entering our middle school—I guessed that the current state of their children's backpacks was a hot mess. (They usually laughed, both with recognition and at a principal talking about "a hot mess.") Having students work on Chromebooks means a swift end to the jumble of paper that buries tomorrow's homework, last week's test, and September's study guide. Students never, ever lose their Chromebooks, which means that they always have the materials they need. The dog never eats the homework when it's on the Chromebook! Adults use electronic tools to keep themselves organized; Chromebooks can remove a huge organizational barrier to student progress. This doesn't affect what historians Tyack and Cuban (1995) call "the familiar grammar of schooling": teachers still assign and collect work and decide and distribute instructional materials. But technology can make those familiar pathways run a lot more smoothly.

That familiar grammar—how school looks, the basic setup—can also, through technology, be far more responsive to student needs. English grammar is one example. Our English teachers used NoRedInk for student grammar practice. This is the familiar exercise of correcting sentences, but through an opening survey, NoRedInk identifies both topics of interest and areas of weakness for each student. The technology allows one student to correct sentence fragments about Taylor Swift while the student next to her fixes subject-verb agreement about soccer. No teacher could make 25 different grammar worksheets for each class. But a computer can—and can correct them instantly, providing immediate feedback. Technology has the power to eliminate trade-offs: in this case, between individual attention to students and the realities of teacher workload. After all, improving students' writing and letting teachers rest are both core values; a human grading student homework is not!

Personalizing instruction in a deep sense is really, really hard. (I'll get to that.) But personalizing practice should fit the way schools are already organized and improve activities schools already do. For math homework, rather than problems to review in class the next day, we assigned online practice through software that offered immediate corrections, additional practice, and tips when students struggled. (Teachers could also see, before class, the common areas of challenge.) Similarly, for summer work, we assigned our students math and reading practice, with individual pathways through a variety of online programs (including differentiated reading at each student's level). We were able to easily check their activity online throughout the summer and contact parents when children weren't working. Our students experienced no summer learning loss, and, compared to national norms, they grew by five percentile points in math and two percentile points in reading from June to September (using NWEA's Measures of Academic Progress). This addressed a huge issue in American education—and it wouldn't be possible without the Chromebooks and the personalized practice platforms. These are small steps. But remember that small steps are powerful.

This summer work was a small step, but it felt like a big decision. The previous year, we'd assigned a single middle-grade novel as summer reading. Other schools in our city did the same. A unifying book, or a summer book list, has social legitimacy; parents expect it, and teachers and students understand it. That's true whether kids read books on the list or speed through the one required novel during the last weekend in August, or whether teachers, in the onslaught of the start of school, ever actually read or grade the response essay. The teachers, overwhelmed their first week back, don't value the essay. And why should they? It's a common structure but not a core value. The core values, at least for us, were that students continue to read during the summer and avoid a summer-long setback in math skills. We could use technology to better achieve those core values if we left the old structure behind.

At the core of teaching and learning, though—the interaction of curriculum, teacher, and students—"Does it have to be this way?" is a harder question. Do all students have to do the exact same grammar practice or math homework? Technology makes it possible to answer: obviously not. But do all students have to learn the same curriculum, with the same teacher? Technology can, indeed, enable us to take that bigger step. When we stop asking merely, "How can we help students with technology?" and instead ask, "How can we alter the fundamentals of what we do?" we create new models of what a class is, its specific learning purposes, and clear actions for teachers.

Remember the anthropological lens: learning is a fundamental, universal human activity. School is not. Young humans often learn through apprenticeship, by imitating skilled role models. They also learn by exploring what interests and motivates them, whether they build a fort in a forest (my son's favorite activity on Cub Scout campouts) or build a castle in Minecraft (his favorite activity outside Cub Scout campouts!). At my school, we asked how we could use the most up-to-date technology to imitate these older forms of learning. Rather than teaching a curriculum to a class, we created a class that unbound student learning from what the teacher knew, the curriculum dictated, or the rest of the students needed. In this student-led inquiry elective, students could choose what they wanted to learn from online resources. The curriculum was a set of benchmarks, from proposal to final project, to help students structure and stay on track with their learning. The teacher modeled how to plan and follow through on goals for learning but didn't teach any content. And both the teachers and the students loved it. The students learned everything from architecture to the ukulele to languages nobody else in the school knew (including Korean, Hebrew, and Quechua). More broadly, they learned how to learn—they decided what they cared about, planned their learning, and identified online resources that would help. That is, of course, what much of their learning for the rest of their lives will look like.

Their future nonschool learning won't, in other words, look like most of the rest of their secondary school experience. At my innovative school, other classrooms, even the best, looked much like other classrooms have for decades. LCD projectors in front of teachers replaced whiteboards (which replaced chalkboards), and Chromebooks in front of students replaced photocopies (which replaced mimeographs, which replaced, if you go back far enough, slates). In most places, our 1:1 technology was not enough to overcome the interdependent grammar of school as it has been. In most places, teachers continue to provide the resources and the teaching, basically within traditional (and state-mandated) subject areas, and students continue to learn the same things in basically the same ways as other students and as their parents before them.

Technology can help those same ways work marginally better. Common elements of frustration, such as student organization and effective practice, are helped by 1:1 programs. (Though another common element of frustration—distracted students—can be worse!) But technology won't change a school, or education, without other, harder changes, like how we think about teaching, what students should learn, and how we organize classrooms.

In a science fiction future, there will still be a role for teachers and for curriculum: adults to guide students and particular things we want them to learn. But if we imagine education in the year 2150, it's hard to picture classrooms of twenty-five students all learning the same thing at the same time. As familiar as that grammar is, it's possible to move beyond. It doesn't have to be this way.

DON'T FORGET

People created our approach to education, and people can create it anew. The school as we know it is only one of many possibilities. You can open your mind to other possibilities when you look at any aspect of your school and ask, "Does it have to be this way?"

- Opening your mind is hard to do because of the pressures to conform to what everyone else is doing. Beware of social legitimacy; just because it's how others do it doesn't mean it's the right thing to do.
- One way to expand your possibilities is to look beyond current practices and see the core values at stake. Use integrative thinking to create new structures that avoid some trade-offs.
- You can also see learning through an anthropological lens. How would a society without schools approach this challenge? What's actually constant across human history, and what have other societies done in other ways?
- Look for ways education is likely to change (for the better!) in the future. Then take small steps to make that future happen now.

KNOW YOURSELF

Social legitimacy is powerful, but so is your own experience. Just like parents often question any pedagogy that doesn't fit how they were taught, you might find it hard to imagine giving students a different experience than you got. Be aware, and beware, of your history.

- When you were a student, what aspects of school worked for you? Did they work for other students in the same way?

- When you were a student, what aspects of school did you find pointless, boring, or unfair? Does the school you lead replicate those practices?

- What powerful out-of-school learning experiences did you have as a child? Why did they work so well? How can you use those experiences to rethink your school?

- Have you experienced formal education outside of the U.S. system—whether in this country through homeschooling or alternative schools, or in other countries? What was most different? How could those differences be applied within your school?

- Have you ever studied or thought about childhood learning in other times or other cultures? Have you studied the history of American education? What can you recognize as artificial—and therefore changeable—in your school?

- What frustrates you most about your school now? How would other stakeholders—parents, children, teachers, staff—answer that question? Does it have to be that way?

WHAT IF I'M WRONG?

You now have four steps, four questions to ask yourself, that will lead you to the right path and away from bad decisions. You can avoid being wrong if you

1. Find what you're missing.
2. Take small steps.
3. Be aware of trade-offs.
4. Recognize when it doesn't have to be this way.

These steps can be conscious, employed when you know you're at a turning point. But they are better as habits: patterns of thought that you trace repeatedly until your mind turns to them unconsciously. It's hard, though. Our unconscious minds often, automatically, with the best intentions, lead us wrong.

They don't lead us wrong all the time, of course. But we as school leaders often face especially difficult problems, so remember what Daniel Kahneman (2011) said: "when faced with a difficult question, we often answer an easier one instead, usually without noticing the substitution" (p. 12). By definition, when we are wrong, we have no idea that we are wrong. If we did, we'd change our minds, and we'd now be right! Instead, when we make a mistake, we tend to plow forward, unaware of how much deeper into the woods we're getting, unaware of when the cliff edge is right in fr—

You're wrong more often when you're tired. You're wrong more often when you're hungry. You're wrong more often when you're frustrated or depressed or overwhelmed—anytime you don't have top-notch deliberative resources to bring to a problem. And sometimes you're wrong even when you're rested, well-fed, happy, and thoughtful. Invariably, sometimes you're just wrong. You can ask all the right questions, follow all the right steps, and still make the wrong decision.

So what if you're wrong?

THE WRONG PATH: LOSING AT THE CONFIDENCE GAME

Picture the principal at the front of an assembly, quieting an auditorium of unruly kids with an authoritative signal. Picture the principal at the front of a faculty meeting, unfurling directives, armed with ready answers to the few (and timidly asked) questions. Picture the principal front and center, always clear, always sure, always right.

This principal is a fantasy: the battle leader on a white horse, sword in hand, always charging forward. It's a fantasy from Hollywood, where leaders, whether in *Braveheart* or *Lean on Me*, swing a big stick and can solve any problem within two hours. It's a fantasy from early childhood—where we imagine that adults' infallibility is limitless—and early adulthood—where we hope, when the going gets tough, that the *real* grown-ups can swoop in, direct and cool as Batman, and save the day.

It's not just a fantasy, though. I've seen this principal in real life. And I've seen him, and her, implode: formerly right answers need to be revoked a couple weeks later, without a coherent plan, and the shaken faculty realizes just how few clothes the emperor is actually wearing. It usually takes half a year. And at the end of the year, these principals slink off,

CONTINUED

leaving someone else to pick up the pieces. Often, unfortunately, they reappear at another school just as confident—at least in September—as they appeared before.

Don't be this principal. As appealing as it might seem to project total confidence at the September faculty meetings, remember what comes out at the other end of the year. The projection of overconfidence stems, every time, from insecurity and fear. The principal whose style and authority rest on having all the right answers is a principal whose authority will inevitably be undermined, and the bluster exists because, deep down, the principal knows the fall is coming. A leader who relies on authoritative bluster, the presentation of confidence, doesn't have a lot of other tools, like designing systems, empowering teams, or managing change. This principal's answers can be quick and definitive because the questions, and their implications, aren't really understood; such leaders don't know what they don't know. They're examples of what psychologists have named the **Dunning-Kruger effect**: low-skilled people tend to radically overestimate their skills because they don't have a clear idea of what expertise actually looks like. High-skilled people tend to underestimate their skill: they accurately see how complex the world is, and they're a bit overawed by that complexity! You might say, "OK, I won't be this principal—that's not me." But beware. Professor Dunning himself says, "The first rule of the Dunning-Kruger club is you don't know you're a member of the Dunning-Kruger club" (Resnick, 2019, para. 6).

In the rest of this chapter, you'll learn how to resign from the club rather than resign from the principalship, because the answer isn't—can't be—not to lead. Instead, it's to project confidence with a firmer base than the fantasy that you have all the right answers. Sometimes you'll be wrong. And if you've prepared yourself, and your staff, for that unavoidable eventuality, your leadership won't be revealed as weak, and you won't have to slink away at the end of the year. Instead, both you and your school will emerge from wrongness in a stronger place.

Humility and Confidence

As educators, we should be more OK with wrongness; we face it all the time with children. The best teachers see wrongness as foundational and see error as an exemplary teachable moment. They know trying is good, a sign of an active mind; only the withdrawn student who refuses to engage is unable to be wrong. Error, when made explicit, is useful; it's an opportunity to understand misconceptions, to lay bare thinking, to move forward with a new analysis. While good teachers know it's important to call error what it is, to clarify for both individual students and the class as a whole what's actually true, they do so without criticism or shame. "We all make mistakes," these teachers say, and in the best classrooms, the students know it too.

We are ready to laugh at know-it-alls when they are children; we recognize how impossible it is to get all that much right. So how have we, as adults, arrived at the mental place where we subconsciously equate excellence with infallibility? As leaders especially, why do we care so much about how right we are? In her book *Being Wrong*, Kathryn Schulz (2010) describes our equation of error with death: "Certain mistakes can actually kill us, but many, many more of them just make us want to die. That's why the word 'mortify' comes up so often when people talk about their errors. . . . Describing the moment of realizing certain mistakes, we say that we wanted to crawl into a cave, or fall through a hole in the floor, or simply disappear. And we talk about 'losing face,' as if our mistakes really *did* cause us to disappear—as if our identity was rubbed out by the experience of being wrong" (p. 26). In this way of thinking, if you want to exist, you have to be right. To buy into this mindset is to be the mark in a confidence game you're playing on yourself; when the card trick is played out, the game is over, and you have nothing left. If your identity as a leader, and your argument for why others should trust you, is contingent upon mastery, then neither you nor those you lead have any reason to trust your leadership once you, inevitably, stumble.

The flip side of this misplaced authority is the underconfident leader: the equivalent of that withdrawn student hoping not to be noticed. Those who become principals don't share the personality characteristics of that silent student; it's hard to get the job if you actually never say anything. But there is an equivalent type of leader who has learned, unfortunately, to never say anything *definitive*. Take one principal I knew. At the end of his one-on-one meetings, the people he talked to always thought he agreed with them on divisive issues. That is, until after a different one-on-one meeting with a different colleague, when the first colleague heard he'd switched sides. In fact, he never took a side; he didn't have the confidence to make a stand. Another principal I knew would listen to her leadership team propose paths forward, make sure someone took careful notes of the options, and move on to the next item on the agenda. The proposals never resurfaced. Nobody made decisions. The school's problems festered. Schools need leadership, and leadership requires deciding.

The leader who never decides might seem the opposite of the leader who decides too quickly and imagines he is always right. But they work (or don't) from the same flawed model of leaderly confidence—where any lack of authority undermines the claim to leadership. The model looks like a bubble. For the overconfident leader, the bubble is just waiting to pop; for the underconfident leader, it already has.

The right way to approach your inevitable wrongness is to match **humility and confidence**. Humility comes from knowing that you don't have all the answers, that you won't get it all right, that, like everyone, you have your limitations and blind spots. So where does confidence come from? It comes from values and process. Values: you are clear on what you believe and on what you want for your students and community; your confidence is in your vision. Process: you are working in thoughtful ways to achieve your vision, and you have processes both to get as close to "right" as possible and to recognize, confront, and improve where you go wrong.

The best thing I ever said as principal was when my school grew and moved to a new building. As we held August faculty meetings, with construction ongoing and still-packed boxes everywhere, my mantra became "We'll figure it out together." We even printed it on a bumper sticker—and staff members actually put that sticker on their cars. As principal, I got plenty of things wrong (more on that below), but this was something I got right. That's not because it emphasized my lack of error, but because it conveyed my values and my process: collaboration, hard work, and trust that problems, while inevitable, would be overcome. It was a slogan for both humility and confidence.

Back when we asked, "What am I missing?" I introduced you to the superforecasters, those foxlike amateurs whose predictions about the future consistently beat self-styled experts. Remember that humility was a key aspect of their skill. Philip Tetlock writes about them: "The humility required for good judgment is not self-doubt—the sense that you are untalented, unintelligent, or unworthy. It is *intellectual* humility. It is a recognition that reality is profoundly complex, that seeing things clearly is a constant struggle, when it can be done at all, and that human judgment must therefore be riddled with mistakes. This is true for fools and geniuses alike. So it's possible to think highly of yourself and be intellectually humble. In fact, this combination can be wonderfully fruitful. Intellectual humility compels the careful reflection necessary for good judgment; confidence in one's abilities inspires determined action" (Tetlock & Gardner, 2015, pp. 228–229). A different version of the same balance is described by business leader

Ray Dalio (2017), who encourages you to "sincerely believe that you might not know the best possible path and recognize that your ability to deal well with 'not knowing' is more important than whatever it is you do know" (p. 188). For both Tetlock and Dalio, the determined action, or the dealing well, is the point: leadership comes from recognizing that you don't have all the answers and having the decisiveness and skill to move forward anyway.

There's a lot that's scary about school leadership. A core of confidence based on values and process can make mistakes less frightening. Leaders who are unafraid to be wrong project and rely on a core of **emotional stability**. They don't get a temporary false high from their own power or success; they don't feel shaken by their own mistakes or others' differing opinions. Emotional stability can be helped by therapy or medication (many principals have used both!), but in the high-intensity tumult of a school leader's day, emotional stability is that moment of pause when emotions get intense. We can all feel the shame of losing face or the desire to crawl into a hole when we're wrong; we can all feel irritation when someone pushes back or disagrees. Emotionally stable leaders pause with that feeling, mindful of that emotion and how to move strategically forward; they use the pause to decide, consciously, what to do next rather than shrink away or blow up. They re-center and move forward.

I've coached leaders to pause quite literally in these moments and allow silence to settle rather than say something that doesn't get them where they want to go. The pause allows leaders to adjust to the surprise of realized or perceived wrongness and make space for calmer decision making, and it conveys to staff consideration and stability. A leader who takes the time to think through what was said before responding or a leader who is quiet amid the tumult is far preferable to a leader who backpedals, covers her tracks, or lashes out. That's true even if the emotional intensity of some interactions is great enough that the pause—or at least the decision about any next step—needs to last until the next day!

After that mindful pause to show and hopefully feel stability amid wrongness, the best way to move forward is to **accept responsibility and fix it**. Your entire worldview and sense of self don't have to change; you just have to admit that, in this case, you were wrong. For as little as such admissions happen, they're shockingly easy and effective. One psychologist who has studied the phenomenon explains that people fear their competence will be questioned when they admit errors, but that's actually rare. Instead, people who acknowledge their wrongness appear more community-minded and helpful (Resnick, 2019). There are few more powerful demonstrations of leadership than standing up in front of your staff, looking them in the eye, and saying, "I was wrong." You show true strength and build trust by acting transparently. When you display your wrongness—something that others might hide—your colleagues can trust that you tell them the truth. And you show that you won't crumble, that you are strong and secure enough not to worry about a little mistake.

You also set an example. You are showing that your school is the kind of place where mistakes are OK; you are modeling emotional security; you are giving staff members an example of humility and confidence. This can transfer, through your teachers, to your students. This is the essence of public leadership: the leader is visible and must embody the mission and direction of the school. You should take the opportunity to model how to look people in the eye and accept responsibility. Wrongness makes for teachable moments.

A teachable moment is one thing; actually learning from it is another. In my second year as principal, I made a series of big mistakes: external hires for my leadership team who didn't work out. They were good people and bad fits, resulting from a range of errors, including not listening to a negative reference, a haphazard hiring process, and not being clear about the demands of the job. I tried to make things work with each of them, but before long, I realized that I couldn't let my desire to be right in my hiring decisions overwhelm the truth. Halfway through the year, two of these hires were gone. At the end of the year, another was off the team.

If a hire isn't going to work, the earlier you can move on, the better. The first step was to figure out why I'd made these mistakes. (I'd hired these people, so the hiring wasn't *their* fault.) I analyzed my process and asked for feedback from other members of the leadership team; I sought out mentors and talked to them about what I'd done. After that, we formalized interview steps and questions for prospective leaders (as we previously had for teachers); we pushed for more internal leadership development and hires, who wouldn't be surprised by what they were getting into; and I never again ignored a negative reference. Fixing it, in this case, couldn't mean going back in time or even undoing the mistakes I'd made. Instead, I had to learn from being wrong and make that learning explicit.

Meetings: Can We Be Less Wrong Together?

When I told my staff, and put on a bumper sticker, "We'll figure it out together," I meant that inspirationally. I didn't mean literally; my intention was not that we'd sit down, all 100-plus of us, and talk it through. I am not a big fan of meetings, especially really big meetings.

Like a lot of folks who enjoy getting things done, my dislike of meetings stems from what often feels like their wastefulness. Meetings seem slow and inefficient in a job where time is always of the essence. They seem that way, in part, because so many meetings feel pointless. Why do this many people need to be gathered in this room for this long? Does it really have to be this way?

The truth is, many meetings don't need to exist, or exist in the way they do. Their purpose is to share information, which could be done by e-mail; they last an hour when they could be 20 minutes; they recur weekly when every two weeks would be enough. These flaws belong to the leader who called the meeting or allowed it to exist. You've seen it before: someone sits at the head of the table and stumbles through an agenda, and others slouch with a computer open, doing other work, participating with half a mind. They know such a meeting doesn't require their full attention.

I hope you don't have half-minded people on your team. I hope you have open-minded people, and I hope that you get the most out of your encounters with them. The best purpose of meetings is for constructive disagreement among smart, caring people. Ray Dalio argues for what he calls **radical open-mindedness**, which is not just an admission that you might be wrong, but a bias toward the possibility that others have better ideas than you do. This is radical because it is so counter to our normal psychology, in which, as Kathryn Schulz (2010) describes, "a whole lot of us go through life assuming that we are basically right, basically all the time, about basically everything: about our political and intellectual convictions, our religious and moral beliefs, our assessment of other people, our memories, our grasp of facts. As absurd as it sounds when we stop to think about it, our steady state seems to be one of unconsciously assuming that we are very close to omniscient" (p. 4). When we realize the absurdity of this, we also realize that increased reliance on other people is the only way to make up for our own inadequacies. Open-minded people circle around to ask, continually, "What am I missing?"

If you build a culture of open-mindedness and enter meetings with an issue for real discussion, meetings can be a way to strategically avoid wrongness. As Dalio (2017) writes, "A few good decision makers working effectively together can significantly outperform a good decision maker working alone—and even the best decision maker can significantly improve his or her decision making with the help of other excellent decision makers" (p. 198). Such improvement relies on strong facilitation and a mutual dedication to radical open-mindedness. Meetings should be exercises in differing perspectives. You can, after all, make better decisions when you see what you'd been missing.

When I visit schools, what kind of meeting I'm observing is often clear before the meeting starts based on where the leader sits: at the head of the table or in the middle? The head of the table signifies control, with a flow of ideas downward; the purpose of the meeting is for the leader at the head to tell the rest of the attendees what's what. If other attendees have something to share, the channel just reverses, with information flowing from the rest of the table to the head. On the other hand, if the leader sits in the middle of the table, she likely sees her role as facilitation, or managing a flow that works more like a network, with cross-cutting channels and connections made sideways. The leader is still a leader, but from the center: the heart, not the head. Such a meeting is likely to be more talkative and more collaborative. If you believe in radical open-mindedness, which I do, it's also less likely to end up wrong. Kathryn Schulz (2010) describes "some ways we can try to prevent mistakes. We can foster the ability to listen to each other and the freedom to speak our minds. We can create open and transparent environments instead of cultures of secrecy and concealment. And we can permit and encourage everyone, not just a powerful inner circle, to speak up when they see the potential for error. These measures might be a prescription for identifying and eliminating mistakes, but they sound like something else: a prescription for democracy" (p. 311).

The *we* in Schulz's prescription is the *we* of leadership. Leadership should be humble and confident enough to believe that the leader doesn't have a monopoly on truth. Radical open-mindedness is democratic, but that doesn't mean decision making needs to be—most things in a school shouldn't be put to a vote! Instead, it is democratic in the sense that varied voices are allowed, heard, and taken seriously. In other words, good meetings matter. Procedurally, one option is a suggestion from Nobel Prize winner Daniel Kahneman (2011): "before an issue is discussed, all members of the committee should be asked to write a very brief summary of their position." He explains that "the standard practice of open discussion gives too much weight to the opinions of those who speak early and assertively, causing others to line up behind them" (p. 85). If everyone starts with an independent judgment and shares it, the group, and the leader, can get the benefit of everyone's open mind. Again, that doesn't mean a vote; at least, it doesn't have to. The decision itself can remain with the leader as long as nobody is expecting a vote—discussions should always begin with clarity on how a decision will be made—and as long as the leader shows that he has truly listened and explains his rationale.

Even with a better discussion protocol, groupthink can dominate. Multiple people can be wrong together, all missing the same things! One solution is to **mandate dissent**. Caroline Webb (2016) offers two useful strategies: appoint a devil's advocate tasked to find the best counterarguments for the unpopular side, and ask everyone involved to speculate on provocative questions such as, "If there were a completely different way to see this, what would it be?" These are time-consuming approaches, which will make already long meetings that much longer. But when decisions are big enough—like expulsions, high-dollar purchases, or leadership hires—the trade-off is worth it.

Approaches like this, focused on transparency and diverse opinions, have buy-in value on their own. Most people are fine with a leader deciding (they don't want the responsibility or the possible blame for being wrong!) as long as they feel heard. If you are wrong after what's perceived as a fair process, you can still sustain your core functions as a leader: to uphold values and to create strong process. Chip and Dan Heath, in their book *Decisive* (2013), call this **procedural justice**: the sense among stakeholders that the process was fair, even if they disagree with the outcome. If that sense is strong, even those who didn't get what they wanted can feel satisfied. What if you're wrong? That's a lot better, it turns out, than if you're unfair.

Experience: What We Learn from Wrongness

In *Being Wrong*, Kathryn Schulz (2010) argues that we have the wrong idea about wrongness: rather than fearing error, we should value its educational potential. "Wrongness is a vital part of how we learn and change," she says. "Thanks to error, we can revise our understanding of ourselves and amend our ideas about the world" (p. 5). As educators, we know this; every time we have students correct their errors on a test, or revise a marked-up paper, we act on it. But as educators, we also know that there's little more frustrating than repeated wrongness. When the student makes the same error over and over again, we feel—at least, *I* feel—a sense not just of wrongness, but of being *wronged*; the world isn't supposed to work like this. We are supposed to learn from experience; what we go through is supposed to have an effect. You might have heard of this as the 10,000-hour rule, Malcolm Gladwell's (2008) theory that expertise, in fields from hockey to violin, is the result of 10,000 hours of practice. If you work 60 hours a week as principal, in other words, for 50 weeks a year, you'll be an expert principal in three and a half years!

The bad news is, others—including Anders Ericcson, the psychological researcher Gladwell cited in his book—disagree with the 10,000-hour rule. And it's easy to see why, in the case of principals and the three-and-a-half-year-rule. In those 60 hours a week, you're balancing a budget, calling back parents, observing classrooms, rearranging lunch duty, mediating two students, and picking up trash. These aren't one activity in which to become expert. The actual route to expertise, according to Ericsson (Ericsson, Krampe, & Tesch-Romer, 1993), is deliberate practice over an extended period of time (more like ten years). Note that **deliberate practice** consists of activities done for the purpose of practice and improvement, as opposed to regular work, public performance, or other activities in which the purpose is not practice and improvement. You certainly aren't picking up trash as practice to improve your level of trash pickup! When we practice, part of our intention is to catch and fix errors; we focus on the aspects where we most need improvement. That's what makes the practice deliberate. But as principal, you're often just trying to get things done.

This perspective—how crowded our life is as we remake our errors—can help us empathize with that wrong-again student. The student who makes the same error over and over isn't actually repeating the exact same error. The words in the math problem are different even if the function is the same; the context for the punctuation has changed, though the comma's absence hasn't. The student, like the overwhelmed principal, looks at a world of constant change, without a fixed point of reference; she can't find the pattern amid the noise. When she made her last error, it was just one moment in a busy day. There was nothing deliberate about it and no moment to deliberately learn from it.

And yet, eventually, she learns. When new principals ask me, with circles under their eyes, stress-eating Doritos at 3 p.m. for lunch, "Will it ever get easier?" this is the hope I can offer: you do gain expertise over time, and you learn faster when you **deliberately look for patterns**. This parent complaint is like that other parent complaint; how did you deal with it last time? This August professional development is like last August's professional development; drag the old agenda out from the folder where you saved it. That teacher evaluation meeting didn't go well; identify where it went wrong and make a note for next time.

Experts are experts because they deal with variations on the same situations over and over. Good plumbers know where the blockage is because they've seen so many similar pipes; good doctors know what the pain means because they've heard so many similar complaints. In *Streetlights and Shadows* (2009), Gary Klein calls this the **recognition-primed decision model**: the essence of expertise is the ability to understand a situation through recognition. The quickly accurate decisions an experienced firefighter or surgeon can make are a function of having seen so many fires or open wounds. (And experienced principals have probably seen both!) These decisions are often unconscious, because recognition primes the expert mind to decide a course of action before the conscious mind proceeds with rational thought. That's why, as Klein explains, firefighters locate danger zones in a burning building without knowing why; the voice of experience speaks so quickly that consciousness can't keep up.

After your first year as principal, you have already done the first day of school, back-to-school-night, parent–teacher conferences, and rounds of teacher evaluation, scheduling, and hiring; and while each year of these have their own permutations, the recognition-primed decision model will allow you to make quicker decisions every time. But beware two common errors. First, if you've made the wrong decision once, a quicker decision will just be a quicker *wrong* decision unless you've identified the error and made a change. Consciousness—that is, mindfulness—matters; you have to turn errors into occasions for deliberate practice if you don't want to repeat them. Second, you have to know what's being repeated and what isn't. If you've figured out how to deal with one parent requesting a teacher switch, you can repeat that strategy again and again. But if the third parent is the first to complain of gender discrimination, you can't allow the recognition-primed decision model to take over. On the other hand, if you see every single situation—every parent meeting, every kid scuffle, every time the building's Wi-Fi sputters—as totally unique, you can't learn; your third year might as well be your first. The key is to look for elements you recognize and then ask what you might be missing.

Experience helps if you learn from it, and expertise, in limited, recognition-primed ways, is possible. It will get easier. But humility is more important than expertise; expertise can grow through humility, but if you think you're an expert (remember the Dunning-Kruger effect), both your humility and your performance will suffer! Even experts need to ask themselves key questions at every step to keep themselves honest and to avoid too much wrongness. The best school leaders, like the best teachers, are not the ones who are right most often. The best school leaders are the most humane. So what if they're wrong sometimes? It's better to be wise than right.

Don't Forget

As thoughtful a leader as you might be, you'll still make mistakes. Your approach toward those inevitable errors will shape your leadership, your relationships, and your school.

- Any leadership that depends on unquestioned authority is fragile.
- The projection of absolute self-confidence covers up insecurity, and leaders who try to mask their fear with bluster are inevitably found out.
- Treat wrongness by adults, including yourself, as you would mistakes by children: as opportunities for learning.

CONTINUED

- Because mistakes are inevitable, humility is the key to effective leadership. When you know you don't have all the answers, and you'll sometimes be wrong, you show a deeper confidence that your core values and thoughtful process will get you, and your school, through the hard times.
- Even with the best process, you'll still make mistakes. And when you do, project—and aim to feel—emotional stability. Those you lead will watch to see whether you're shaken or resolute. A moment's pause conveys and creates emotional stability.
- Accept responsibility and fix the error. When you accept responsibility, you seem more trustworthy and worthy of confidence, and you model the behavior you want in others (including students). Fixing the error includes both making it right and figuring out why you made it in the first place so you can avoid it the next time around.
- Radically open-minded meetings are one way to be less wrong. Another way to avoid errors is experience, which depends on the recognition-primed decision model. You can deliberately look for patterns and see the resemblance between your current challenge and situations you've faced before. If you were right the first time, you can be right again; if you were wrong before, and took the opportunity to learn, that deliberate practice can help you improve.

KNOW YOURSELF

When people are wrong, they describe the feeling as wanting to hide, disappear, or even die. None of those are a good option for school leaders! Consider how you can deal with the possibility, and inevitable reality, of your own wrongness.

- When you picture a confident leader, what do you see? Where does that confidence come from?
- When you picture a humble leader, what do you see? Would your colleagues describe you as humble? How would you feel if they did?
- How much do your own mistakes affect your emotional stability? How much do you display emotional stability to others? What would happen in your school if your own emotional stability increased or decreased?
- When was the last time you took responsibility for a mistake? What happened? What would happen if you did so more often?
- With that last error, do you know why you were wrong? Have you changed your procedures to reduce the likelihood of being wrong next time?
- Would you describe your decision-making process as democratic? How do you foster useful dissent? When others disagree with you, do they feel procedural justice has been achieved?
- If you are a new leader, how can you learn from your mistakes? If you are an experienced leader, what situations have you been able to treat like repetitions of those you've seen before, and when has that approach gotten you in trouble?
- How much compassion do you show for others when they are wrong? Can you try to feel more compassion for yourself?

Conclusion

You're Not Alone

As I write this conclusion, I'm in a text message exchange about where to meet tonight for dinner. It's the beginning of the school year, and the texts are from the principal who succeeded me, formerly my assistant principal. She's in the middle of new teacher orientation. I'm sitting in a coffee shop with my computer. I'm eager to catch up on school news. I suspect she's eager for a whiskey!

We get together when we can, for stories and laughter, and for advice that goes both ways. That's a pattern (minus the whiskey) we established when we worked together every day: catch up, try to relax for a few minutes, and help each other figure out the path forward. Pauses and mindfulness are easier in a coffee shop than in the tumult of a school, but they're possible in a school too. They're a lot more possible if others redirect you—push you, sometimes— toward that mindful path. My former assistant principal and I didn't start with this relationship. We had to consciously make it, with small steps, realizing what we were missing and, sometimes, telling each other when we were wrong.

Like other leaders at the school I used to lead, the assistant principal (now principal) is brilliant, compassionate, and wise.

And I left confident in the members of the leadership team's ability to decide without me. My confidence when I left, in other words, stemmed in part from the humility I tried to lead with. I didn't have all the information; I wasn't always right; many decisions weren't mine. Sure, there were lots of new challenges for my assistant principal when she removed the *assistant* part. But to her, decision making for the school wasn't new.

Good leaders make good decisions. Great leaders teach others to decide for themselves. This is some of the core work of coaching a leadership team. And it's not different from the core work of coaching yourself to make better decisions. The work is to ask your team members, over and over, until the neural pathways made by these questions become the new normal:

- What are you missing?
- What's one small step?
- Where's the trade-off?
- Does it have to be this way?
- What if you're wrong?

You work with your team to build the humility implied by these questions in a way that still allows, and requires, a decision to be made. By doing so, you build confidence for action while encouraging self-awareness about inevitable limitations.

This shift, from asking yourself these questions to asking them of others, requires attention to tone. Imagine asking a supervisee, "What if you're wrong?" (Or imagine your boss saying it to you!) Depending on the relationship, it might sound confrontational or even accusatory. It might prompt defensiveness or hurt feelings. Helping others learn to make their own path requires a distinct approach; it calls on trust and vulnerability. If a supervisor admits that she is sometimes wrong, and clarifies that the world won't end if *you* are, then the question "What if you're wrong?" feels a lot different than being asked it by an all-knowing taskmaster. And when asked that question by a supervisor who offers confidence enough to empower you with decision-making authority, such confidence changes the tone and even the relationship.

Too often leaders treat team building as a distinct activity, an afternoon outing during a week otherwise devoted to professional development. A ropes course or bowling alley can be fun—I've taken teams there—but they don't create the culture of teamwork that you need. There are people who want and care about such activities, and you have to take their desires seriously, but these activities don't lead to change. Instead, true team building is about building the habits for real, shared work and asking, "How do we move forward in this complex world?"

A team can help each other with the reflective practices in this book. A team, the more diverse the better, can help uncover what any one person might be missing. A team can identify and track small steps, can locate trade-offs, can brainstorm beyond the way things have been. A team can tell the truth, and offer support when any one member turns out to be wrong. The truth is difficult to find and sometimes difficult to hear. Teams are paths for perspective-taking and perspective-changing, and they are the heart of leadership.

The life of a leader is grueling, often exhausting. It's crucial to find the right people and build a team; that can make leadership less lonely. The stress and tumult of school leadership, like other experiences of shared intensity, can build incredibly strong bonds. That's true even if the way you organize your team is just to divide up responsibilities. But divided teams are both less fun and less effective. A team can help each other and push each other forward to a better place.

Decision making should be a shared burden. Collective responsibility is a lighter weight to carry, and it's a better path when built together.

ACKNOWLEDGMENTS

Leadership is a team effort. I'm grateful and lucky that I've learned alongside these teams: Alice Deal Middle School, American University School of Education, Cesar Chavez Public Charter Schools, Community Day Charter School, DC Public Schools, DC International School, IDEA Public Charter School, Schoolkit, and Washington Leadership Academy. I also learned from great teachers at the Harvard Graduate School of Education, especially Chris Dede, Karen Mapp, and Linda Nathan, and about leadership from Mario Giardiello and Melissa Martin.

On the team for this book: Rob Adelberg, Seth Andrew, Nancy Aries, Megan Doyle, Dean Harris, Susan Hills, Stacy Kane, Ruth Kaplan, Michael Kavanagh, Justin Lessek, Melody Maitland, Brian Pick, Josie Rodberg, Juliet Ross, Pankti Sevak, Andrea Sparks-Brown, Maya Stewart, Joey Webb, Nicole Welsh, and Yolanda Young. They're not responsible for what's missing or for any places I'm wrong, but they made it better.

Portions of this work were previously published, in different form, in the magazines *Educational Leadership*, *Harvard Business Review*, *Principal*, and *Principal Leadership*.

All stories in the book are true. Some names and identifying details have been changed.

School leadership takes an emotional toll. The school leader's family may get the worst of that toll! My wife, Alison MacAdam, put up with early mornings, late nights, and far too much stress, and still loved me and supported my dreams. This book is dedicated to her.

REFERENCES

Barahona-Corrêa, J. B., & Filipe, C. N. (2016). A concise history of Asperger syndrome: The short reign of a troublesome diagnosis. *Frontiers in Psychology, 6*(2024). https://doi.org/10.3389/fpsyg.2015.02024

Berger, P. (2005, October 25). Thomas Edison's crystal ball: A contrarian on education's brave new silicon world. *Education Week, 25*(09), 44–45.

Brint, S. (2017). *Schools and societies.* Redwood City, CA: Stanford University Press.

Christensen, C. M., Horn, M. B., & Johnson, C. W. (2008). *Disrupting class: How disruptive innovation will change the way the world learns.* New York: McGraw-Hill.

Dalio, R. (2017). *Principles: Life and work.* New York: Simon & Schuster.

Ericcson, K. A., Krampe, R. T., & Tesch-Romer, C. (1993). The role of deliberate practice in the acquisition of expert performance. *Psychological Review, 100*(3), 363–406.

Gaskins, S., & Paradise, R. (2010). Learning through observation in daily life. In D. F. Lancy, J. Bock, & S. Gaskins (Eds.). *The anthropology of learning in childhood* (pp. 85–118). Walnut Creek, CA: AltaMira Press.

Gilliam, W. S., Maupin, A. N., Reyes, C. R., Accavitti, M., & Shic, F. (2016, September 28). *Do early educators' implicit biases regarding sex and race relate to behavior expectations and recommendations of preschool expulsions and suspensions?* New Haven, CT: Yale Child Study Center.

Gladwell, M. (2008). *Outliers: The story of success.* New York: Little, Brown.

Guskey, T. (2015). *On your mark: Challenging the conventions of grading and reporting.* Bloomington, IN: Solution Tree.

Heath, C., & Heath, D. (2013). *Decisive: How to make better choices in life and work*. New York: Currency.

Heymann, J. (2010). *Profit at the bottom of the ladder: Creating value by investing in your workforce*. Boston: Harvard Business Review Press.

IDEO. (2012). *Design thinking for educators*. Retrieved from https://designthinkingforeducators.com/

Jena, A. B., Barnett, M., & Layton, T. J. (2018, November 28). The link between August birthdays and A.D.H.D. *New York Times,* p. A31.

Johnson, S. (2018). *Farsighted: How we make the decisions that matter most*. New York: Riverhead Books.

Kahneman, D. (2011). *Thinking, fast and slow*. New York: Farrar, Straus & Giroux.

Klein, G. (2009). *Streetlights and shadows: Searching for the keys to adaptive decision making*. Cambridge, MA: MIT Press.

Milner, R. (2015). *Rac(e)ing to class: Confronting poverty and race in schools and classrooms*. Cambridge, MA: Harvard Education Press.

Project Implicit. (n.d.). Frequently asked questions: Might my preference for one group over another be a simple ingroup preference? Author. Retrieved from https://implicit.harvard.edu/implicit/faqs.html

Resnick, B. (2019, June 26). An expert on human blind spots gives advice on how to think. *Vox*. Retrieved from https://www.vox.com/science-and-health/2019/1/31/18200497/dunning-kruger-effect-explained-trump

Riel, J., & Martin, R. L. (2017). *Creating great choices: A leader's guide to integrative thinking*. Boston: Harvard Business Review Press.

Schmoker, M. (2016). *Leading with focus: Elevating the essentials for school and district improvement*. Alexandria, VA: ASCD.

Schulz, K. (2010). *Being wrong: Adventures in the margin of error*. New York: Ecco.

Stewart, C. (2018, December 17). I'm here for restorative justice practices until your son punches my daughter at school. *Citizen Ed*. Retrieved from https://citizen.education/2018/12/17/im-here-for-restorative-justice-practices-until-your-son-punches-my-daughter-at-school/

Tetlock, P., & Gardner, D. (2015). *Superforecasting: The art and science of prediction*. New York: Crown.

Tyack, D., & Cuban, L. (1995). *Tinkering toward utopia: A century of public school reform*. Cambridge, MA: Harvard University Press.

Webb, C. (2016). *How to have a good day: Harness the power of behavioral science to transform your working life*. New York: Crown Business.

INDEX

ABOUT THE AUTHOR

Simon Rodberg is a strategy consultant and leadership coach who teaches educational leadership at American University. He was the founding principal of DC International School, a public charter school in Washington, D.C., as well as an assistant principal, district official, and teacher in D.C. and Massachusetts. His school was among the top performers among the city, earning "best middle school" and "best high school" in the *Washington City Paper* poll and other accolades. His writing has appeared in *Educational Leadership*, *Harvard Business Review*, *Principal Leadership*, *Principal* magazine, and the *New York Times*. You can contact him at simon.rodberg@gmail.com or @simonrodberg on Twitter.